Unapologetically Authentic. Own That Damn Business.

Business Mindset Vibe Guide

Sara Entzel

HOW TO **USE THIS** LIKE A
DAMN BUSINESS BADASS

This isn't just some damn workbook — it's a full-blown **mindset rebellion**.

You didn't show up to play it safe, shrink yourself, or build someone else's boring-ass version of success. You're here to own your **power**, take up **space**, and **build** a business that's bold, aligned, and **UNAPOLOGETICALLY YOU.**

The She's the Strategy™ Business Mindset Workbook is your ride-or-die space to think big, plan with fire, and rise into the fierce woman you've always known you were.

Inside, you'll get:

- ✅ **Business Snapshot:** Your no-BS foundation for starting or refining a brand that actually feels like you.

- ✅ **Weekly Planners:** Structure your days like a business badass — without the burnout or corporate fluff.

- ✅ **Journaling Prompts:** Ditch the mental junk, rewrite the script, and tap into your next-level mindset.

- ✅ **Reflection Pages:** Track your wins, celebrate your growth, and extract the gold from every badass lesson.

This isn't about grinding harder or pretending to be someone you're not. It's about stepping into the full, loud, magnetic force that is you.

Say the bold thing. Take up all the space. Lead loud. Live big. Fuck playing small.

You are the **strategy.**
You are the **brand.**
You are the **damn business badass.**

Let's build it.

Sara Entzel

Creator of She's the Strategy™

HOW TO **COMPLETE THIS** LIKE A
DAMN BUSINESS BADASS

CHOOSE YOUR FLOW
(aka: How to Actually Get This Shit Done)

Listen, babe — there's no one right way to rock this book. Your journey, your rules. But if you're looking for a little guidance (and a big ol' permission slip), here it is. Let's cut the crap — you've got two ways to tackle this badass book:

Option 1: The "Fuck It, Let's GO" Approach
Total immersion = total badass energy.
Pour yourself a fat glass of wine, lock the damn door, and dive in.
Give yourself 1–2 uninterrupted hours to get in the zone, blast through it, and let all that brilliance pour out.

Option 2: The "Bite-Size Boss" Method
Short on time? No worries.
Commit to 2 pages a day, 6 days in a row.
Each page should take about 15 minutes or less — so block off 25–30 minutes daily.
Perfect for the babes who like to marinate in the magic without feeling rushed.

MAKE A DAMN DATE WITH YOUR DESTINY.
Mark the day (or days) you're committing to show the hell up for yourself and finish this book.

> Block the time.
> Protect it like your future depends on it — because it literally does.
> No flaking. No ghosting yourself. No "oops I forgot."

You are not hoping to make moves — you're choosing it. Sharpie that shit in like it's non-negotiable (because it IS). This is you setting the tone for every badass thing you're about to create. Your future self is watching. Make her proud as fuck.

MONday	**TUES**day	**WEDNES**day	**THURS**day	**FRI**day	**SATUR**day	**SUN**day

You ready? (Hell yeah, you are.)

BUSINESS SNAPSHOT LIKE A
DAMN BUSINESS BADASS

BUSINESS NAME + TAGLINE

BUSINESS NAME: _____

TAGLINE / SLOGAN: _____
(WHAT'S YOUR VIBE IN ONE LINE?)

FOUNDER INFORMATION

NAME: _____

TITLE: _____

CEO MISSION STATEMENT (IN ONE SENTENCE):

"I HELP _____ DO _____ SO THEY CAN _____ ."

BUSINESS CATEGORY / INDUSTRY

(EX: COACHING, SERVICE-BASED, PRODUCT-BASED, DIGITAL MARKETING, HEALTH & WELLNESS, REAL ESTATE, ETC.)

PRODUCTS, SERVICES, OR OFFERS. LIST WHAT YOU PROVIDE:

TARGET AUDIENCE / IDEAL CLIENT DEMOGRAPHICS:

AGE RANGE:	LOCATION:	GENDER IDENTITY:
WHAT ARE THEY STRUGGLING WITH?	WHAT DO THEY DREAM OF HAVING?	WHAT ARE THEY SEARCHING FOR THAT YOU PROVIDE?

3 WORDS OR PHRASES THAT DESCRIBE MY BUSINESS

_____

_____

She's the
STRATEGY
Unapologetically Authentic. Own That Damn Business.

BUSINESS SNAPSHOT LIKE A
DAMN BUSINESS BADASS

CORE VALUES
(HOW YOU DO BUSINESS + HOW YOU MAKE PEOPLE FEEL)

VALUE #1	VALUE #2	VALUE #3

MARKETING & VISIBILITY

MAIN PLATFORMS I USE: (Ig, Fb, Tiktok, Email, Linkedin, Website, Networking, Etc.) _____

WHERE MY IDEAL CLIENTS FREQUENT: (Hangout Spots, Events, Networking) _____

MONEY & GROWTH GOALS

MONTHLY REVENUE GOAL	YEARLY REVENUE GOAL	DREAM INCOME LEVEL

PERSONAL FREEDOM GOAL (EX: TRAVEL, TIME, SUPPORT): _____

THINGS I NO LONGER TOLERATE IN BUSINESS: _____

PROSPECTIVE BUSINESS HOURS

MON	TUE	WED	THU

FRI	SAT	SUN	

She's the **STRATEGY**
Unapologetically Authentic. Own That Damn Business.

DEFINING YOUR CORE VALUES LIKE A
DAMN BUSINESS BADASS

Defining your core values is like setting the damn GPS for your business — without them, you're just driving in circles hoping you don't crash.

Your values are your non-negotiables, your internal compass, your "hell yes" and "hell no" filter. They keep you grounded when shit gets chaotic and guide every decision, from the clients you take on to the offers you create.

And let's be clear — this isn't about picking some generic buzzwords to slap on your website. It's about digging deep and owning what actually matters to you. Integrity? Freedom? Impact? Whatever your flavor, your business should live and breathe those values in everything it does. Because when you're rooted in what you truly stand for, you stop chasing success — and start building it on your damn terms. Core values aren't fluff. They're your business ride-or-dies.

WHY YOU DO WHAT YOU DO — AND HOW YOU WANT IT TO FEEL.

WHAT 3 VALUES GUIDE THE WAY I SERVE, LEAD, AND SHOW UP?

HOW DO I WANT MY CLIENTS OR AUDIENCE TO FEEL WHEN THEY INTERACT WITH MY BRAND?

WHERE HAVE I NOT BEEN LIVING MY VALUES — AND WHAT SMALL SHIFT COULD BRING ME BACK INTO ALIGNMENT?

WHAT BOUNDARIES SUPPORT ME IN HONORING THESE VALUES?

DEFINING YOUR IDENTITY LIKE A
DAMN BUSINESS BADASS

Defining your identity in business is not about fitting into someone else's polished-ass box — it's about building something that screams you from the inside out. Your brand, your vibe, your voice — it should all reflect who the hell you actually are, not who you think you need to be to be taken seriously. Because let's be real: trying to blend in is the fastest way to burn out. When you own your quirks, your fire, your values, and your story, you attract the right people, repel the wrong ones, and run a business that feels aligned as fuck.

Your identity isn't just your logo or colors — it's the energy behind everything you say and do. So define it loud, live it proud, and stop diluting your magic to make other people comfortable. You weren't made to blend in. You were made to stand the hell out.

WHAT **HABITS** DO I NEED TO EMBODY TO BECOME HER?

WHAT AM I **NO LONGER AVAILABLE FOR** IN THIS NEW VERSION OF MYSELF?

HOW DOES THE **CEO VERSION** OF ME THINK, ACT, AND SPEAK?

THINK:

ACT:

SPEAK:

SOUL GOAL SETTING LIKE A
DAMN BUSINESS BADASS

Soul goal setting isn't about forcing yourself to hit some random-ass milestone that looks good on paper but feels like crap in your body. It's about setting goals that light you up from the inside out — goals that feel like a full-body YES. The kind that are rooted in purpose, not pressure. Vision, not validation. These aren't goals you set to prove something to the world — they're the ones that pull you forward, because they're aligned with who the hell you are and what you're really here to do.

So screw the hustle-for-hustle's-sake vibe. This is about creating a vision that honors your energy, your truth, and your damn soul. And when your goals feel that real and that aligned? You don't have to force motivation, you become the momentum. Set the goals that make your heart race, your gut say "hell yes," and your higher self smirk like "finally." That's how you build something worth showing the fuck up for.

SETTING GOALS WITH SOUL
WHAT ARE MY TOP 3 PRIORITIES THIS SEASON (LIFE + BUSINESS)?

LIFE #1	LIFE #2	LIFE #3

BUSINESS #1	BUSINESS #2	BUSINESS #3

WHAT WOULD SUCCESS FEEL LIKE IN 3 MONTHS?

IF I LET GO OF PEOPLE-PLEASING, WHAT WOULD I PURSUE UNAPOLOGETICALLY?

She's the
STRATEGY
Unapologetically Authentic. Own That Damn Business.

RITUALS + ROUTINES LIKE A
DAMN BUSINESS BADASS

Rituals and routines aren't about being some rigid, color-coded calendar queen (unless that's your jam — then slay on). They're about creating sacred structure in your day that fuels your power, not drains it. It's less "wake up at 5AM and drink celery juice" and more "what the hell does my soul need to stay grounded, lit up, and unstoppable?"

Whether it's journaling with your coffee, blasting 90's punk rock before sales calls, or checking in with your goals like it's a damn love letter — your rituals are what anchor your energy and keep you aligned when the chaos hits.

Consistency isn't about being perfect — it's about showing up, again and again, for yourself. Your routines don't need to look like anyone else's. They just need to work for you. Because when you lead your day with intention instead of reaction? You stop surviving and start running shit.

So build the rituals that make you feel like the CEO of your own damn energy. And then protect them like the boundaries boss you are.

THE ENERGY AND HABITS BEHIND THE BRAND.

WHAT ARE 3 HABITS THAT DRAIN MY ENERGY OR PULL ME OUT OF ALIGNMENT — AND NEED TO BE RELEASED?

1

2

3

WHAT MORNING OR WEEKLY RITUALS HELP ME FEEL GROUNDED AND POWERFUL?

WHAT SMALL HABIT COULD I START TODAY THAT ALIGNS ME WITH SUCCESS?

She's the
STRATEGY
Unapologetically Authentic. Own That Damn Business.

CONFIDENCE & VISIBILITY LIKE A
DAMN BUSINESS BADASS

Confidence and visibility go hand in hand — and if you're waiting to feel ready before you show up, you're gonna be waiting forever, babe. Confidence isn't something you're magically born with — it's something you build every damn time you choose to be seen, even when your voice shakes or your inner critic's screaming, "Who the hell do you think you are?" (Spoiler: you're a badass, that's who.)

VISIBILITY isn't vanity — it's leadership. It's saying, "I believe in what I do enough to let the world fucking see it." Your people can't find you if you're hiding behind perfection, procrastination, or fear. Show up messy. Show up scared. Show up real. Just SHOW UP.

CONFIDENCE comes from doing the damn thing, not from thinking about it. So go ahead — take up space, speak your truth, post the thing, pitch the offer, and let your magic be seen. You weren't made to blend in. You were made to shine like the bold, brilliant force you already are.

WHAT DOES THE MOST CONFIDENT, VISIBLE VERSION OF ME DO ON A REGULAR BASIS — AND HOW CAN I START DOING JUST 1 OF THOSE THINGS NOW?

WHERE AM I **DIMMING MY LIGHT**, PLAYING SMALL, OR HOLDING BACK — AND WHY?

_____

_____

_____

WHAT **PROOF** DO I ALREADY HAVE THAT I CAN DO HARD THINGS?

_____

_____

WHAT'S MY **VISIBILITY EDGE** RIGHT NOW?
(The one thing that makes your stomach flip just thinking about it — that's where your growth lives.)

She's the
STRATEGY
Unapologetically Authentic. Own That Damn Business.

MONEY MINDSET LIKE A
DAMN BUSINESS BADASS

Money mindset? Babe, it's not just about numbers — it's about energy, worth, and how damn willing you are to own your value. If you're constantly undercharging, overgiving, or feeling guilty about making bank, guess what? That's not strategy — that's self-sabotage in a cute outfit. Shifting your money mindset means dropping the shame, smashing those old stories ("money is bad," "I'm not good with money," "who would pay that?"), and deciding that wealth gets to feel aligned, abundant, and fun as hell.

You're not greedy for wanting more — you're a woman with vision. And money in the hands of a purpose-driven woman? That's a damn revolution. So raise your rates, own your brilliance, and stop apologizing for wanting to get paid. You're not just building a business — you're building a legacy. And legacies? They deserve to be well-funded, baby.

MONEY MINDSET REWIRE
WHERE AM I UNDERCHARGING, OVERGIVING, OR UNDERVALUING MYSELF — AND WHY?

UNDERCHARGING	OVERGIVING	UNDERVALUING MYSELF

WHAT BELIEFS AROUND MONEY DID I INHERIT THAT NO LONGER SERVE ME?

HOW DO I WANT TO FEEL WHEN I RECEIVE MONEY IN MY BUSINESS?

WHAT DOES **FINANCIAL FREEDOM** LOOK LIKE FOR ME — AND WHY DOES IT **MATTER?**

She's the
STRATEGY
Unapologetically Authentic. Own That Damn Business.

MEETING RESISTANCE LIKE A
DAMN BUSINESS BADASS

IMPOSTER SYNDROME & **INNER CRITIC WORK**
BECAUSE EVERY BOLD WOMAN MEETS RESISTANCE.

Meeting resistance? Good. That means you're getting close to something big. Resistance shows up like clockwork when you're about to break through your comfort zone and do something that actually matters. It'll whisper shit like "Who do you think you are?" or "Maybe later," or "Let's just scroll TikTok instead."

But here's the truth: resistance isn't a stop sign — it's a signal. A flashing neon "you're onto something powerful" sign. So don't freak out when it hits. Breathe through it. Call it out. And then keep fucking going.

Because the ones who make it? They don't wait for the resistance to disappear — they move with it, work through it, and let it sharpen them. Resistance isn't your enemy. It's proof you're growing. So show up anyway, shake shit up, and remind yourself — you were built for this.

WHAT PROOF DO I HAVE THAT I AM CAPABLE AND POWERFUL?

WHAT **STORY AM I TELLING MYSELF** ABOUT NOT BEING **"READY"** OR **"QUALIFIED"**? _____
_____
_____

WHERE IN MY BUSINESS (OR LIFE) AM I CURRENTLY FEELING THE **MOST RESISTANCE?**
_____
_____

IF I COULD TALK TO MY **IMPOSTER VOICE**, WHAT WOULD I SAY TO HER?

FAILURE HAPPENING LIKE A
DAMN BUSINESS BADASS

Failure in business? Oh honey, it's not just normal — it's necessary. If you're not failing, you're probably playing way too damn small. Every misstep, flop, or WTF moment is actually a goldmine in disguise — packed with lessons, redirections, and a whole lot of growth.

The key? Stop treating failure like a dirty word. Instead, take that shit with grace, learn what you need to learn, and keep it moving. Cry if you need to, scream into a pillow, cuss a little (or a lot), but then get up, fix your focus, and get back in the game. Because the women who win? They don't avoid failure — they dance with it, learn from it, and come back sharper, bolder, and even more unstoppable. Failure isn't the opposite of success — it's the fast track to it.

REFRAMING THE STORY
FAILURE ISN'T A SIGN THAT YOU'RE NOT CUT OUT FOR THIS. IT'S A SIGNAL THAT SOMETHING NEEDS TO EVOLVE. AND EVOLUTION IS WHAT CEOS DO.

INSTEAD OF: "I failed."
SAY: "I learned something I wouldn't have if I played it safe."

INSTEAD OF: "Nobody bought."
SAY: "This wasn't the right message for the right people — yet."

INSTEAD OF: "I should have known better."
SAY: "Now I do know better. Let's go."

WHAT STORY AM I TELLING MYSELF ABOUT FAILURE? AND WHAT STORY DO I WANT TO WRITE INSTEAD?

WHAT WOULD I DO DIFFERENTLY NEXT TIME (WITH NO SHAME, JUST STRATEGY)?

WHAT DIDN'T GO THE WAY I WANTED — AND HOW DOES IT ACTUALLY MAKE ME STRONGER?

WHAT WOULD MY FUTURE CEO SELF SAY TO ME RIGHT NOW?

CELEBRATE WINS LIKE A
DAMN BUSINESS BADASS

MAKING WINS PART OF YOUR IDENTITY.

Celebrate your damn wins — ALL of them. Not just the big, shiny, Instagram-worthy ones. I'm talking about the baby steps, the mindset shifts, the "I didn't quit today" moments. Because every time you pause to celebrate, you're rewiring your brain to see your own badassery.

And let's be real — if you're always racing to the next goal without taking a damn second to say "HELL YES, I did that," you're missing the whole fucking point.

Celebration is how you build momentum. It's how you anchor progress. It's how you remind yourself that you're not just working hard — you're growing, evolving, and slaying.

So pop the bubbly, dance around your office, buy the fancy coffee, shout yourself out in your journal — whatever feels like a YES to your soul. Just don't skip it. You are not "too busy" to witness your own magic. This journey deserves to be celebrated loud, proud, and often. Because YOU are the damn win.

WHAT'S A RECENT RESULT OR BREAKTHROUGH I'VE BEEN DOWNPLAYING — AND HOW CAN I HONOR IT INSTEAD?

_____

_____

_____

_____

WHAT DID I DO TODAY THAT MY PAST SELF WOULD'VE BEEN DAMN PROUD OF?

WHAT DID I ACCOMPLISH IN MY LIFE THAT I'M PROUD OF (BIG OR SMALL)?

WHAT'S ONE SMALL CELEBRATION RITUAL I CAN MAKE A REGULAR PART OF MY LIFE OR BUSINESS?

CREATING YOUR MANIFESTO LIKE A
DAMN BUSINESS BADASS

WRAP IT ALL UP WITH A
POWERFUL DECLARATION!

Creating your manifesto is like writing a love letter to your future self — but with fire, f-bombs, and full-body conviction. It's your bold-ass declaration of who you are, what you stand for, and how you're showing the hell up in the world.

No more shrinking, no more second-guessing, no more waiting for permission. Your manifesto is your line in the sand — your "this is who I am, and I'm done playing small" moment. It's not about perfection. It's about power. You get to write the rules. You get to define the vibe. You get to speak your truth louder than the bullshit that's tried to silence you.

So get fierce. Get raw. Get real as hell. This is your rebel call, your energetic blueprint, your reminder that you didn't come here to blend in — you came to disrupt, to lead, and to fucking rise. Write it. Speak it. Live it. And let the world feel every damn word.

I AM THE WOMAN WHO...

I LEAD MY BUSINESS WITH...

I BELIEVE IN...

I AM BECOMING...

I WILL NO LONGER...

YOUR NEXT BOLD MOVE
STARTS HERE

DAILY **JOURNALING** LIKE A
DAMN BUSINESS BADASS

This isn't just a journal page — it's your daily CEO-level check-in.

It's where strategy meets self-awareness.
Where clarity kicks chaos in the ass.
Where you pause, reflect, and remind yourself: I am the damn business badass.

This page is your no-excuses space to reconnect with your mind, body, and business — all in under 10 minutes. Use it each morning like the power ritual it is.

Here's how to use it like the incredible bitch you are:

START WITH YOUR STATE

Get brutally honest about your energy, motivation, and capacity. Because pushing through like a robot isn't leadership — it's burnout waiting to happen. Grace > grit.

GRATITUDE REWIRES YOUR BRAIN

List 3 things you're damn grateful for. Doesn't matter if it's your coffee or closing a six-figure deal. Big or small — gratitude keeps your vibe high and your power turned on.

REFLECT ON YESTERDAY

Did you show up like the badass you are? Cool. If not? No shame — just shift.
Check those boxes, then use the space to figure out what you're doing differently today.
That's growth, baby.

SET INTENTIONS WITH CLARITY

Drop 3 needle-moving action steps that align with your vision and fuel your momentum.
They don't need to be big. They just need to be intentional as fuck.

DAILY REMINDER

End with a truth bomb or affirmation. What do you need to hear today?
Say it loud. Write it down. Own that shit.

Pro Tip: Do this every damn weekday for 21 days and watch your energy, confidence, and clarity hit new heights. This isn't just action. It's embodiment. It's evolution.

You've got this.

HOW WAS MY **SLEEP LAST NIGHT**

① ② ③ ④ ⑤ ⑥ ⑦ ⑧ ⑨ ⑩

HOW **MOTIVATED** DO I FEEL TODAY

① ② ③ ④ ⑤ ⑥ ⑦ ⑧ ⑨ ⑩

WHERE IS MY **PHYSICAL ENERGY LEVEL**

① ② ③ ④ ⑤ ⑥ ⑦ ⑧ ⑨ ⑩

HOW IS MY **EMOTIONAL CAPACITY**

① ② ③ ④ ⑤ ⑥ ⑦ ⑧ ⑨ ⑩

SHITTY ————————————————— AWESOME

THREE THINGS I'M **GRATEFUL FOR:**

_____
_____
_____
_____
_____
_____
_____

REFLECTION OF YESTERDAY

DID I DO THE THINGS I **COMMITED** TO DO? Ⓨ Ⓝ

DID I DO SOMETHING FOR **MYSELF**? (joy, rest, movement, fun) Ⓨ Ⓝ

DID I PROTECT MY **ENERGY** AND SET **CLEAR BOUNDARIES**? Ⓨ Ⓝ

DID I **CELEBRATE** A SMALL WIN (or acknowledge progress) Ⓨ Ⓝ

DID I CHECK IN WITH MY **VISION + GOALS** (even briefly)? Ⓨ Ⓝ

DID I MAKE AT LEAST ONE **BOLD MOVE** OR **CEO DECISION**? Ⓨ Ⓝ

DID I **STAY FOCUSED** ON MY GROWTH? Ⓨ Ⓝ

IF I ANSWERED "NO" TO ANY **WHAT DO I SHIFT TODAY**?

_____
_____
_____
_____
_____

---

3 ACTION STEPS (COMMITMENTS) I WILL DO TODAY
THINGS YOU WILL COMMIT TO YOURSELF AND YOUR BUSINESS TO SUPPORT YOUR VISION

SOMETHING I NEED TO **REMIND MYSELF** OF TODAY _____

BUSINESS TO DO LIST:

PERSONAL TO DO LIST:

TOP PRIORITIES TODAY

_____

_____

_____

_____

HOW MUCH **TIME** WILL I DEDICATE TO MY BUSINESS TODAY?

6 am

7 am

8 am

9 am

10 am

11 am

12 pm

1 pm

2 pm

3 pm

4 pm

5 pm

6 pm

7 pm

HOW WAS MY **SLEEP LAST NIGHT**

(1) (2) (3) (4) (5) (6) (7) (8) (9) (10)

HOW **MOTIVATED** DO I FEEL TODAY

(1) (2) (3) (4) (5) (6) (7) (8) (9) (10)

WHERE IS MY **PHYSICAL ENERGY LEVEL**

(1) (2) (3) (4) (5) (6) (7) (8) (9) (10)

HOW IS MY **EMOTIONAL CAPACITY**

(1) (2) (3) (4) (5) (6) (7) (8) (9) (10)

SHITTY ———————————————— AWESOME

THREE THINGS I'M
GRATEFUL FOR:

_____
_____
_____
_____
_____
_____

REFLECTION OF YESTERDAY

	Y N
DID I DO THE THINGS I **COMMITED** TO DO?	(Y)(N)
DID I DO SOMETHING FOR **MYSELF**? (joy, rest, movement, fun)	(Y)(N)
DID I PROTECT MY **ENERGY** AND SET **CLEAR BOUNDARIES**?	(Y)(N)
DID I **CELEBRATE** A SMALL WIN (or acknowledge progress)	(Y)(N)
DID I CHECK IN WITH MY **VISION + GOALS** (even briefly)?	(Y)(N)
DID I MAKE AT LEAST ONE **BOLD MOVE** OR **CEO DECISION**?	(Y)(N)
DID I **STAY FOCUSED** ON MY GROWTH?	(Y)(N)

IF I ANSWERED "NO" TO ANY
WHAT DO I SHIFT TODAY?

_____
_____
_____
_____

3 **ACTION STEPS** (COMMITMENTS) I WILL DO TODAY
THINGS YOU WILL COMMIT TO YOURSELF AND YOUR BUSINESS TO SUPPORT YOUR VISION

SOMETHING I NEED TO **REMIND MYSELF** OF TODAY _____

BUSINESS TO DO LIST:

PERSONAL TO DO LIST:

TOP PRIORITIES TODAY

_____
_____
_____
_____

HOW MUCH **TIME** WILL I DEDICATE TO MY BUSINESS TODAY?

6 am

7 am

8 am

9 am

10 am

11 am

12 pm

1 pm

2 pm

3 pm

4 pm

5 pm

6 pm

7 pm

HOW WAS MY **SLEEP LAST NIGHT**

(1) (2) (3) (4) (5) (6) (7) (8) (9) (10)

HOW **MOTIVATED** DO I FEEL TODAY

(1) (2) (3) (4) (5) (6) (7) (8) (9) (10)

WHERE IS MY **PHYSICAL ENERGY LEVEL**

(1) (2) (3) (4) (5) (6) (7) (8) (9) (10)

HOW IS MY **EMOTIONAL CAPACITY**

(1) (2) (3) (4) (5) (6) (7) (8) (9) (10)

SHITTY ——————————————— AWESOME

THREE THINGS I'M
GRATEFUL FOR:

_____
_____
_____
_____
_____
_____
_____
_____

REFLECTION OF YESTERDAY

DID I DO THE THINGS I **COMMITED** TO DO? (Y) (N)

DID I DO SOMETHING FOR **MYSELF**? (joy, rest, movement, fun) (Y) (N)

DID I PROTECT MY **ENERGY** AND SET **CLEAR BOUNDARIES**? (Y) (N)

DID I **CELEBRATE** A SMALL WIN (or acknowledge progress) (Y) (N)

DID I CHECK IN WITH MY **VISION + GOALS** (even briefly)? (Y) (N)

DID I MAKE AT LEAST ONE **BOLD MOVE** OR **CEO DECISION**? (Y) (N)

DID I **STAY FOCUSED** ON MY GROWTH? (Y) (N)

IF I ANSWERED "NO" TO ANY
WHAT DO I SHIFT TODAY?

_____
_____
_____
_____
_____
_____

3 ACTION STEPS (COMMITMENTS) I WILL DO TODAY
THINGS YOU WILL COMMIT TO YOURSELF AND YOUR BUSINESS TO SUPPORT YOUR VISION

SOMETHING I NEED TO **REMIND MYSELF** OF TODAY _____

BUSINESS TO DO LIST:

PERSONAL TO DO LIST:

TOP PRIORITIES TODAY

_____

_____

_____

HOW MUCH **TIME** WILL I
DEDICATE TO MY BUSINESS
TODAY?

6 am

7 am

8 am

9 am

10 am

11 am

12 pm

1 pm

2 pm

3 pm

4 pm

5 pm

6 pm

7 pm

HOW WAS MY **SLEEP LAST NIGHT**

(1)(2)(3)(4)(5)(6)(7)(8)(9)(10)

HOW **MOTIVATED** DO I FEEL TODAY

(1)(2)(3)(4)(5)(6)(7)(8)(9)(10)

WHERE IS MY **PHYSICAL ENERGY LEVEL**

(1)(2)(3)(4)(5)(6)(7)(8)(9)(10)

HOW IS MY **EMOTIONAL CAPACITY**

(1)(2)(3)(4)(5)(6)(7)(8)(9)(10)

SHITTY ——————————————— AWESOME

THREE THINGS I'M **GRATEFUL FOR:**

_____
_____
_____
_____
_____
_____

REFLECTION OF YESTERDAY

DID I DO THE THINGS I **COMMITED** TO DO? (Y)(N)

DID I DO SOMETHING FOR **MYSELF**? (joy, rest, movement, fun) (Y)(N)

DID I PROTECT MY **ENERGY** AND SET **CLEAR BOUNDARIES**? (Y)(N)

DID I **CELEBRATE** A SMALL WIN (or acknowledge progress) (Y)(N)

DID I CHECK IN WITH MY **VISION + GOALS** (even briefly)? (Y)(N)

DID I MAKE AT LEAST ONE **BOLD MOVE** OR **CEO DECISION**? (Y)(N)

DID I **STAY FOCUSED** ON MY GROWTH? (Y)(N)

IF I ANSWERED "NO" TO ANY **WHAT DO I SHIFT TODAY**?

_____
_____
_____
_____
_____

3 ACTION STEPS (COMMITMENTS) I WILL DO TODAY
THINGS YOU WILL COMMIT TO YOURSELF AND YOUR BUSINESS TO SUPPORT YOUR VISION

SOMETHING I NEED TO **REMIND MYSELF** OF TODAY _____

BUSINESS TO DO LIST:

PERSONAL TO DO LIST:

TOP PRIORITIES TODAY

_____

_____

_____

HOW MUCH **TIME** WILL I DEDICATE TO MY BUSINESS TODAY?

6 am

7 am

8 am

9 am

10 am

11 am

12 pm

1 pm

2 pm

3 pm

4 pm

5 pm

6 pm

7 pm

HOW WAS MY **SLEEP LAST NIGHT**

(1) (2) (3) (4) (5) (6) (7) (8) (9) (10)

HOW **MOTIVATED** DO I FEEL TODAY

(1) (2) (3) (4) (5) (6) (7) (8) (9) (10)

WHERE IS MY **PHYSICAL ENERGY LEVEL**

(1) (2) (3) (4) (5) (6) (7) (8) (9) (10)

HOW IS MY **EMOTIONAL CAPACITY**

(1) (2) (3) (4) (5) (6) (7) (8) (9) (10)

SHITTY ————————————————— AWESOME

THREE THINGS I'M **GRATEFUL FOR:**

_____
_____
_____
_____
_____
_____
_____
_____

REFLECTION OF YESTERDAY

DID I DO THE THINGS I **COMMITED** TO DO?   (Y)(N)

DID I DO SOMETHING FOR **MYSELF**? (joy, rest, movement, fun)   (Y)(N)

DID I PROTECT MY **ENERGY** AND SET **CLEAR BOUNDARIES**?   (Y)(N)

DID I **CELEBRATE** A SMALL WIN (or acknowledge progress)   (Y)(N)

DID I CHECK IN WITH MY **VISION + GOALS** (even briefly)?   (Y)(N)

DID I MAKE AT LEAST ONE **BOLD MOVE** OR **CEO DECISION**?   (Y)(N)

DID I **STAY FOCUSED** ON MY GROWTH?   (Y)(N)

IF I ANSWERED "NO" TO ANY **WHAT DO I SHIFT TODAY**?

_____
_____
_____
_____
_____
_____

3 **ACTION STEPS** (COMMITMENTS) I WILL DO TODAY

THINGS YOU WILL COMMIT TO YOURSELF AND YOUR BUSINESS TO SUPPORT YOUR VISION

SOMETHING I NEED TO **REMIND MYSELF** OF TODAY _____

_____

BUSINESS TO DO LIST:

PERSONAL TO DO LIST:

TOP PRIORITIES TODAY

_____

_____

_____

_____

HOW MUCH **TIME** WILL I
DEDICATE TO MY BUSINESS
TODAY?

6 am

7 am

8 am

9 am

10 am

11 am

12 pm

1 pm

2 pm

3 pm

4 pm

5 pm

6 pm

7 pm

She's the STRATEGY
Unapologetically Authentic. Own That Damn Business.

JAN   FEB   MAR   APR   MAY   JUN   JUL   AUG   SEP   OCT   NOV   DEC   20___
1 2 3 4 5 6 7 8 9 10 11 12 13 14 15 16 17 18 19 20 21 22 23 24 25 26 27 28 29 30 31

HOW WAS MY **SLEEP LAST NIGHT**

(1) (2) (3) (4) (5) (6) (7) (8) (9) (10)

HOW **MOTIVATED** DO I FEEL TODAY

(1) (2) (3) (4) (5) (6) (7) (8) (9) (10)

WHERE IS MY **PHYSICAL ENERGY LEVEL**

(1) (2) (3) (4) (5) (6) (7) (8) (9) (10)

HOW IS MY **EMOTIONAL CAPACITY**

(1) (2) (3) (4) (5) (6) (7) (8) (9) (10)

SHITTY ————————————————— AWESOME

THREE THINGS I'M **GRATEFUL FOR:**

_____
_____
_____
_____
_____
_____
_____

REFLECTION OF YESTERDAY

DID I DO THE THINGS I **COMMITED** TO DO?	(Y) (N)
DID I DO SOMETHING FOR **MYSELF**? (joy, rest, movement, fun)	(Y) (N)
DID I PROTECT MY **ENERGY** AND SET **CLEAR BOUNDARIES**?	(Y) (N)
DID I **CELEBRATE** A SMALL WIN (or acknowledge progress)	(Y) (N)
DID I CHECK IN WITH MY **VISION + GOALS** (even briefly)?	(Y) (N)
DID I MAKE AT LEAST ONE **BOLD MOVE** OR **CEO DECISION**?	(Y) (N)
DID I **STAY FOCUSED** ON MY GROWTH?	(Y) (N)

IF I ANSWERED "NO" TO ANY **WHAT DO I SHIFT TODAY?**

_____
_____
_____
_____
_____

3 **ACTION STEPS** (COMMITMENTS) I WILL DO TODAY
THINGS YOU WILL COMMIT TO YOURSELF AND YOUR BUSINESS TO SUPPORT YOUR VISION

SOMETHING I NEED TO **REMIND MYSELF** OF TODAY _____

BUSINESS TO DO LIST:

PERSONAL TO DO LIST:

TOP PRIORITIES TODAY

HOW MUCH **TIME** WILL I DEDICATE TO MY BUSINESS TODAY?

6 am

7 am

8 am

9 am

10 am

11 am

12 pm

1 pm

2 pm

3 pm

4 pm

5 pm

6 pm

7 pm

She's the STRATEGY
Unapologetically Authentic. Own That Damn Business.

JAN   FEB   MAR   APR   MAY   JUN   JUL   AUG   SEP   OCT   NOV   DEC   20___
1 2 3 4 5 6 7 8 9 10 11 12 13 14 15 16 17 18 19 20 21 22 23 24 25 26 27 28 29 30 31

HOW WAS MY **SLEEP LAST NIGHT**
(1)(2)(3)(4)(5)(6)(7)(8)(9)(10)

HOW **MOTIVATED** DO I FEEL TODAY
(1)(2)(3)(4)(5)(6)(7)(8)(9)(10)

WHERE IS MY **PHYSICAL ENERGY LEVEL**
(1)(2)(3)(4)(5)(6)(7)(8)(9)(10)

HOW IS MY **EMOTIONAL CAPACITY**
(1)(2)(3)(4)(5)(6)(7)(8)(9)(10)

SHITTY ——————————————————— AWESOME

THREE THINGS I'M
GRATEFUL FOR:

_____
_____
_____
_____
_____
_____
_____

REFLECTION OF YESTERDAY

DID I DO THE THINGS I **COMMITED** TO DO?   (Y)(N)

DID I DO SOMETHING FOR **MYSELF**? (joy, rest, movement, fun)   (Y)(N)

DID I PROTECT MY **ENERGY** AND SET **CLEAR BOUNDARIES**?   (Y)(N)

DID I **CELEBRATE** A SMALL WIN (or acknowledge progress)   (Y)(N)

DID I CHECK IN WITH MY **VISION + GOALS** (even briefly)?   (Y)(N)

DID I MAKE AT LEAST ONE **BOLD MOVE** OR **CEO DECISION**?   (Y)(N)

DID I **STAY FOCUSED** ON MY GROWTH?   (Y)(N)

IF I ANSWERED "NO" TO ANY
WHAT DO I SHIFT TODAY?

_____
_____
_____
_____
_____

3 **ACTION STEPS** (COMMITMENTS) I WILL DO TODAY
THINGS YOU WILL COMMIT TO YOURSELF AND YOUR BUSINESS TO SUPPORT YOUR VISION

SOMETHING I NEED TO **REMIND MYSELF** OF TODAY _____

BUSINESS TO DO LIST:

PERSONAL TO DO LIST:

TOP PRIORITIES TODAY

_____

_____

_____

_____

HOW MUCH **TIME** WILL I DEDICATE TO MY BUSINESS TODAY?

6 am

7 am

8 am

9 am

10 am

11 am

12 pm

1 pm

2 pm

3 pm

4 pm

5 pm

6 pm

7 pm

WEEKLY CHECK-IN

PERSONAL ENERGY & WELL-BEING
On a scale of 1–10, how would I rate...

MY OVERALL **ENERGY** THIS WEEK

(1)(2)(3)(4)(5)(6)(7)(8)(9)(10)

MY **EMOTIONAL CAPACITY** THIS WEEK

(1)(2)(3)(4)(5)(6)(7)(8)(9)(10)

MY **MOTIVATION + CLARITY** THIS WEEK

(1)(2)(3)(4)(5)(6)(7)(8)(9)(10)

SHITTY ———————————————— AWESOME

WHAT SUPPORTED MY WELL-BEING THIS WEEK?

_____

_____

WHAT DRAINED ME THAT I WANT TO SHIFT OR ELIMINATE?

_____

_____

WHAT DID I DO JUST FOR ME THIS WEEK?

_____

_____

BUSINESS & LEADERSHIP REFLECTIONS

DID I **STAY FOCUSED** ON MY TOP PRIORITIES? (Y)(N)

DID I **LEAD** WITH CONFIDENCE, EVEN WHEN IT WAS HARD? (Y)(N)

DID I **SHOW UP** FOR MY BRAND IN A WAY I'M PROUD OF? (Y)(N)

DID I COMMUNICATE **CLEAR BOUNDARIES** AROUND MY TIME? (Y)(N)

WHAT WORKED REALLY WELL IN MY BUSINESS THIS WEEK?

_____

WHAT CHALLENGES CAME UP, AND WHAT DID I LEARN FROM THEM?

_____

WHAT BOLD MOVE DID I MAKE (OR WISH I HAD)?

_____

ALIGNMENT & INTENTION

AM I STILL MOVING TOWARD MY BIGGER VISION — OR AM I JUST STAYING BUSY?

WHAT DO I NEED TO PAUSE, PIVOT, OR RELEASE RIGHT NOW?

WHAT'S ONE THING I WANT TO RECOMMIT TO NEXT WEEK?

NEXT WEEK'S FOCUS

ONE BOLD THING I'LL DO THIS WEEK

ONE BOUNDARY I'LL PROTECT

WEEKLY **GOAL PLANNER** LIKE A
DAMN BUSINESS BADASS

MY **WEEKLY** FOCUS
TOP 3 POWER GOALS FOR THIS WEEK - (WHAT ACTUALLY MOVES THE NEEDLE — NOT BUSY WORK.)

ENERGY + MINDSET FOCUS:

(ONE VIBE, MANTRA, OR ENERGY YOU'RE CHOOSING TO LEAD WITH THIS WEEK.) _____

CELEBRATE YOUR DAMN WINS:

INNER WINS **(MINDSET + ENERGY)**	**ACTION WINS** **(SH*T YOU ACTUALLY DID)**	**ALIGNMENT WINS** **(SOUL-LEVEL YES MOMENTS)**
THE MOMENTS YOU CHOSE GROWTH, CALM, COURAGE, OR CLARITY OVER CHAOS.	TANGIBLE MOVES YOU MADE — BIG OR SMALL — THAT PROVE YOU'RE BUILDING MOMENTUM.	WHEN SOMETHING FELT RIGHT, EASY, ALIGNED, OR JOYFULLY YOU.

WHAT NEEDS TO **SHIFT** ASAP?

She's the
STRATEGY
Unapologetically Authentic. Own That Damn Business.

HOW WAS MY **SLEEP LAST NIGHT**

(1) (2) (3) (4) (5) (6) (7) (8) (9) (10)

HOW **MOTIVATED** DO I FEEL TODAY

(1) (2) (3) (4) (5) (6) (7) (8) (9) (10)

WHERE IS MY **PHYSICAL ENERGY LEVEL**

(1) (2) (3) (4) (5) (6) (7) (8) (9) (10)

HOW IS MY **EMOTIONAL CAPACITY**

(1) (2) (3) (4) (5) (6) (7) (8) (9) (10)

SHITTY ————————————————— AWESOME

THREE THINGS I'M **GRATEFUL FOR:**

_____
_____
_____
_____
_____
_____
_____
_____
_____

REFLECTION OF YESTERDAY

DID I DO THE THINGS I **COMMITED** TO DO?   (Y) (N)

DID I DO SOMETHING FOR **MYSELF**? (joy, rest, movement, fun)   (Y) (N)

DID I PROTECT MY **ENERGY** AND SET **CLEAR BOUNDARIES**?   (Y) (N)

DID I **CELEBRATE** A SMALL WIN (or acknowledge progress)   (Y) (N)

DID I CHECK IN WITH MY **VISION + GOALS** (even briefly)?   (Y) (N)

DID I MAKE AT LEAST ONE **BOLD MOVE** OR **CEO DECISION**?   (Y) (N)

DID I **STAY FOCUSED** ON MY GROWTH?   (Y) (N)

IF I ANSWERED "NO" TO ANY **WHAT DO I SHIFT TODAY**?

_____
_____
_____
_____
_____

3 ACTION STEPS (COMMITMENTS) I WILL DO TODAY
THINGS YOU WILL COMMIT TO YOURSELF AND YOUR BUSINESS TO SUPPORT YOUR VISION

SOMETHING I NEED TO **REMIND MYSELF** OF TODAY _____

BUSINESS TO DO LIST:

PERSONAL TO DO LIST:

TOP PRIORITIES TODAY

HOW MUCH **TIME** WILL I DEDICATE TO MY BUSINESS TODAY?

6 am

7 am

8 am

9 am

10 am

11 am

12 pm

1 pm

2 pm

3 pm

4 pm

5 pm

6 pm

7 pm

HOW WAS MY **SLEEP LAST NIGHT**

① ② ③ ④ ⑤ ⑥ ⑦ ⑧ ⑨ ⑩

HOW **MOTIVATED** DO I FEEL TODAY

① ② ③ ④ ⑤ ⑥ ⑦ ⑧ ⑨ ⑩

WHERE IS MY **PHYSICAL ENERGY LEVEL**

① ② ③ ④ ⑤ ⑥ ⑦ ⑧ ⑨ ⑩

HOW IS MY **EMOTIONAL CAPACITY**

① ② ③ ④ ⑤ ⑥ ⑦ ⑧ ⑨ ⑩

SHITTY ———————————————— AWESOME

THREE THINGS I'M **GRATEFUL FOR:**

_____
_____
_____
_____
_____
_____
_____

REFLECTION OF YESTERDAY

DID I DO THE THINGS I **COMMITED** TO DO?   Ⓨ Ⓝ

DID I DO SOMETHING FOR **MYSELF**? (joy, rest, movement, fun)   Ⓨ Ⓝ

DID I PROTECT MY **ENERGY** AND SET **CLEAR BOUNDARIES**?   Ⓨ Ⓝ

DID I **CELEBRATE** A SMALL WIN (or acknowledge progress)   Ⓨ Ⓝ

DID I CHECK IN WITH MY **VISION + GOALS** (even briefly)?   Ⓨ Ⓝ

DID I MAKE AT LEAST ONE **BOLD MOVE** OR **CEO DECISION**?   Ⓨ Ⓝ

DID I **STAY FOCUSED** ON MY GROWTH?   Ⓨ Ⓝ

IF I ANSWERED "NO" TO ANY **WHAT DO I SHIFT TODAY**?

_____
_____
_____
_____
_____

3 ACTION STEPS (COMMITMENTS) I WILL DO TODAY
THINGS YOU WILL COMMIT TO YOURSELF AND YOUR BUSINESS TO SUPPORT YOUR VISION

SOMETHING I NEED TO **REMIND MYSELF** OF TODAY _____

BUSINESS TO DO LIST:

PERSONAL TO DO LIST:

TOP PRIORITIES TODAY

_____

_____

_____

_____

HOW MUCH **TIME** WILL I
DEDICATE TO MY BUSINESS
TODAY?

6 am

7 am

8 am

9 am

10 am

11 am

12 pm

1 pm

2 pm

3 pm

4 pm

5 pm

6 pm

7 pm

HOW WAS MY **SLEEP LAST NIGHT**

(1) (2) (3) (4) (5) (6) (7) (8) (9) (10)

HOW **MOTIVATED** DO I FEEL TODAY

(1) (2) (3) (4) (5) (6) (7) (8) (9) (10)

WHERE IS MY **PHYSICAL ENERGY LEVEL**

(1) (2) (3) (4) (5) (6) (7) (8) (9) (10)

HOW IS MY **EMOTIONAL CAPACITY**

(1) (2) (3) (4) (5) (6) (7) (8) (9) (10)

SHITTY ——————————————— AWESOME

THREE THINGS I'M **GRATEFUL FOR:**

_____
_____
_____
_____
_____
_____
_____

REFLECTION OF YESTERDAY

DID I DO THE THINGS I **COMMITED** TO DO? (Y) (N)

DID I DO SOMETHING FOR **MYSELF**? (joy, rest, movement, fun) (Y) (N)

DID I PROTECT MY **ENERGY** AND SET **CLEAR BOUNDARIES**? (Y) (N)

DID I **CELEBRATE** A SMALL WIN (or acknowledge progress) (Y) (N)

DID I CHECK IN WITH MY **VISION + GOALS** (even briefly)? (Y) (N)

DID I MAKE AT LEAST ONE **BOLD MOVE** OR **CEO DECISION**? (Y) (N)

DID I **STAY FOCUSED** ON MY GROWTH? (Y) (N)

IF I ANSWERED "NO" TO ANY **WHAT DO I SHIFT TODAY**?

_____
_____
_____
_____
_____

3 **ACTION STEPS** (COMMITMENTS) I WILL DO TODAY
THINGS YOU WILL COMMIT TO YOURSELF AND YOUR BUSINESS TO SUPPORT YOUR VISION

SOMETHING I NEED TO **REMIND MYSELF** OF TODAY _____

BUSINESS TO DO LIST:

PERSONAL TO DO LIST:

TOP PRIORITIES TODAY

HOW MUCH **TIME** WILL I DEDICATE TO MY BUSINESS TODAY?

6 am

7 am

8 am

9 am

10 am

11 am

12 pm

1 pm

2 pm

3 pm

4 pm

5 pm

6 pm

7 pm

HOW WAS MY **SLEEP LAST NIGHT**

(1) (2) (3) (4) (5) (6) (7) (8) (9) (10)

HOW **MOTIVATED** DO I FEEL TODAY

(1) (2) (3) (4) (5) (6) (7) (8) (9) (10)

WHERE IS MY **PHYSICAL ENERGY LEVEL**

(1) (2) (3) (4) (5) (6) (7) (8) (9) (10)

HOW IS MY **EMOTIONAL CAPACITY**

(1) (2) (3) (4) (5) (6) (7) (8) (9) (10)

SHITTY ——————————————————— AWESOME

THREE THINGS I'M **GRATEFUL FOR:**

_____
_____
_____
_____
_____
_____

REFLECTION OF YESTERDAY

DID I DO THE THINGS I **COMMITED** TO DO? (Y)(N)

DID I DO SOMETHING FOR **MYSELF**? (joy, rest, movement, fun) (Y)(N)

DID I PROTECT MY **ENERGY** AND SET **CLEAR BOUNDARIES**? (Y)(N)

DID I **CELEBRATE** A SMALL WIN (or acknowledge progress) (Y)(N)

DID I CHECK IN WITH MY **VISION + GOALS** (even briefly)? (Y)(N)

DID I MAKE AT LEAST ONE **BOLD MOVE** OR **CEO DECISION**? (Y)(N)

DID I **STAY FOCUSED** ON MY GROWTH? (Y)(N)

IF I ANSWERED "NO" TO ANY **WHAT DO I SHIFT TODAY**?

_____
_____
_____
_____
_____

---

3 ACTION STEPS (COMMITMENTS) I WILL DO TODAY

THINGS YOU WILL COMMIT TO YOURSELF AND YOUR BUSINESS TO SUPPORT YOUR VISION

SOMETHING I NEED TO **REMIND MYSELF** OF TODAY _____

BUSINESS TO DO LIST:

PERSONAL TO DO LIST:

TOP PRIORITIES TODAY

_____

_____

_____

_____

HOW MUCH **TIME** WILL I
DEDICATE TO MY BUSINESS
TODAY?

6 am

7 am

8 am

9 am

10 am

11 am

12 pm

1 pm

2 pm

3 pm

4 pm

5 pm

6 pm

7 pm

HOW WAS MY **SLEEP LAST NIGHT**

(1) (2) (3) (4) (5) (6) (7) (8) (9) (10)

HOW **MOTIVATED** DO I FEEL TODAY

(1) (2) (3) (4) (5) (6) (7) (8) (9) (10)

WHERE IS MY **PHYSICAL ENERGY LEVEL**

(1) (2) (3) (4) (5) (6) (7) (8) (9) (10)

HOW IS MY **EMOTIONAL CAPACITY**

(1) (2) (3) (4) (5) (6) (7) (8) (9) (10)

SHITTY ———————————————— AWESOME

THREE THINGS I'M **GRATEFUL FOR:**

_____
_____
_____
_____
_____
_____
_____

REFLECTION OF YESTERDAY

DID I DO THE THINGS I **COMMITED** TO DO? (Y) (N)

DID I DO SOMETHING FOR **MYSELF**? (joy, rest, movement, fun) (Y) (N)

DID I PROTECT MY **ENERGY** AND SET **CLEAR BOUNDARIES**? (Y) (N)

DID I **CELEBRATE** A SMALL WIN (or acknowledge progress) (Y) (N)

DID I CHECK IN WITH MY **VISION + GOALS** (even briefly)? (Y) (N)

DID I MAKE AT LEAST ONE **BOLD MOVE** OR **CEO DECISION**? (Y) (N)

DID I **STAY FOCUSED** ON MY GROWTH? (Y) (N)

IF I ANSWERED "NO" TO ANY **WHAT DO I SHIFT TODAY?**

_____
_____
_____
_____
_____

3 **ACTION STEPS** (COMMITMENTS) I WILL DO TODAY

THINGS YOU WILL COMMIT TO YOURSELF AND YOUR BUSINESS TO SUPPORT YOUR VISION

SOMETHING I NEED TO **REMIND MYSELF** OF TODAY _____

BUSINESS TO DO LIST:

PERSONAL TO DO LIST:

TOP PRIORITIES TODAY

_____

_____

_____

HOW MUCH **TIME** WILL I DEDICATE TO MY BUSINESS TODAY?

6 am

7 am

8 am

9 am

10 am

11 am

12 pm

1 pm

2 pm

3 pm

4 pm

5 pm

6 pm

7 pm

She's the STRATEGY

HOW WAS MY **SLEEP LAST NIGHT**

(1)(2)(3)(4)(5)(6)(7)(8)(9)(10)

HOW **MOTIVATED** DO I FEEL TODAY

(1)(2)(3)(4)(5)(6)(7)(8)(9)(10)

WHERE IS MY **PHYSICAL ENERGY LEVEL**

(1)(2)(3)(4)(5)(6)(7)(8)(9)(10)

HOW IS MY **EMOTIONAL CAPACITY**

(1)(2)(3)(4)(5)(6)(7)(8)(9)(10)

SHITTY ——————————————— AWESOME

THREE THINGS I'M **GRATEFUL FOR:**

_____
_____
_____
_____
_____
_____

REFLECTION OF YESTERDAY

DID I DO THE THINGS I **COMMITED** TO DO? (Y)(N)

DID I DO SOMETHING FOR **MYSELF**? (joy, rest, movement, fun) (Y)(N)

DID I PROTECT MY **ENERGY** AND SET **CLEAR BOUNDARIES**? (Y)(N)

DID I **CELEBRATE** A SMALL WIN (or acknowledge progress) (Y)(N)

DID I CHECK IN WITH MY **VISION + GOALS** (even briefly)? (Y)(N)

DID I MAKE AT LEAST ONE **BOLD MOVE** OR **CEO DECISION**? (Y)(N)

DID I **STAY FOCUSED** ON MY GROWTH? (Y)(N)

IF I ANSWERED "NO" TO ANY **WHAT DO I SHIFT TODAY**?

_____
_____
_____
_____
_____

3 ACTION STEPS (COMMITMENTS) I WILL DO TODAY
THINGS YOU WILL COMMIT TO YOURSELF AND YOUR BUSINESS TO SUPPORT YOUR VISION

SOMETHING I NEED TO **REMIND MYSELF** OF TODAY _____
_____

BUSINESS TO DO LIST:

PERSONAL TO DO LIST:

TOP PRIORITIES TODAY

_____

_____

_____

HOW MUCH **TIME** WILL I DEDICATE TO MY BUSINESS TODAY?

6 am

7 am

8 am

9 am

10 am

11 am

12 pm

1 pm

2 pm

3 pm

4 pm

5 pm

6 pm

7 pm

HOW WAS MY **SLEEP LAST NIGHT**

1 2 3 4 5 6 7 8 9 10

HOW **MOTIVATED** DO I FEEL TODAY

1 2 3 4 5 6 7 8 9 10

WHERE IS MY **PHYSICAL ENERGY LEVEL**

1 2 3 4 5 6 7 8 9 10

HOW IS MY **EMOTIONAL CAPACITY**

1 2 3 4 5 6 7 8 9 10

SHITTY ————————————————— AWESOME

THREE THINGS I'M **GRATEFUL FOR:**

_____

_____

_____

_____

_____

_____

REFLECTION OF YESTERDAY

DID I DO THE THINGS I **COMMITED** TO DO? (Y)(N)

DID I DO SOMETHING FOR **MYSELF**? (joy, rest, movement, fun) (Y)(N)

DID I PROTECT MY **ENERGY** AND SET **CLEAR BOUNDARIES**? (Y)(N)

DID I **CELEBRATE** A SMALL WIN (or acknowledge progress) (Y)(N)

DID I CHECK IN WITH MY **VISION + GOALS** (even briefly)? (Y)(N)

DID I MAKE AT LEAST ONE **BOLD MOVE** OR **CEO DECISION**? (Y)(N)

DID I **STAY FOCUSED** ON MY GROWTH? (Y)(N)

IF I ANSWERED "NO" TO ANY **WHAT DO I SHIFT TODAY**?

_____

_____

_____

_____

_____

---

3 ACTION STEPS (COMMITMENTS) I WILL DO TODAY
THINGS YOU WILL COMMIT TO YOURSELF AND YOUR BUSINESS TO SUPPORT YOUR VISION

SOMETHING I NEED TO **REMIND MYSELF** OF TODAY _____

BUSINESS TO DO LIST:

PERSONAL TO DO LIST:

TOP PRIORITIES TODAY

_____

_____

_____

_____

HOW MUCH **TIME** WILL I DEDICATE TO MY BUSINESS TODAY?

6 am

7 am

8 am

9 am

10 am

11 am

12 pm

1 pm

2 pm

3 pm

4 pm

5 pm

6 pm

7 pm

WEEKLY CHECK-IN

PERSONAL ENERGY & WELL-BEING
On a scale of 1–10, how would I rate...

MY OVERALL **ENERGY** THIS WEEK

(1) (2) (3) (4) (5) (6) (7) (8) (9) (10)

MY **EMOTIONAL CAPACITY** THIS WEEK

(1) (2) (3) (4) (5) (6) (7) (8) (9) (10)

MY **MOTIVATION + CLARITY** THIS WEEK

(1) (2) (3) (4) (5) (6) (7) (8) (9) (10)

SHITTY —————————————————— AWESOME

WHAT SUPPORTED MY WELL-BEING THIS WEEK?

_____

_____

WHAT DRAINED ME THAT I WANT TO SHIFT OR ELIMINATE?

_____

_____

WHAT DID I DO JUST FOR ME THIS WEEK?

_____

_____

BUSINESS & LEADERSHIP REFLECTIONS

DID I **STAY FOCUSED** ON MY TOP PRIORITIES?　(Y) (N)

DID I **LEAD** WITH CONFIDENCE, EVEN WHEN IT WAS HARD?　(Y) (N)

DID I **SHOW UP** FOR MY BRAND IN A WAY I'M PROUD OF?　(Y) (N)

DID I COMMUNICATE **CLEAR BOUNDARIES** AROUND MY TIME?　(Y) (N)

WHAT WORKED REALLY WELL IN MY BUSINESS THIS WEEK?

_____

WHAT CHALLENGES CAME UP, AND WHAT DID I LEARN FROM THEM?

_____

WHAT BOLD MOVE DID I MAKE (OR WISH I HAD)?

_____

ALIGNMENT & INTENTION

AM I STILL MOVING TOWARD MY BIGGER VISION — OR AM I JUST STAYING BUSY?

WHAT DO I NEED TO PAUSE, PIVOT, OR RELEASE RIGHT NOW?

WHAT'S ONE THING I WANT TO RECOMMIT TO NEXT WEEK?

NEXT WEEK'S FOCUS

ONE BOLD THING I'LL DO THIS WEEK

ONE BOUNDARY I'LL PROTECT

WEEKLY **GOAL PLANNER** LIKE A
DAMN BUSINESS BADASS

MY **WEEKLY** FOCUS
TOP 3 POWER GOALS FOR THIS WEEK - (WHAT ACTUALLY MOVES THE NEEDLE — NOT BUSY WORK.)

ENERGY + MINDSET FOCUS:

(ONE VIBE, MANTRA, OR ENERGY YOU'RE CHOOSING TO LEAD WITH THIS WEEK.)

CELEBRATE YOUR DAMN WINS:

INNER WINS **(MINDSET + ENERGY)**	**ACTION WINS** **(SH*T YOU ACTUALLY DID)**	**ALIGNMENT WINS** **(SOUL-LEVEL YES MOMENTS)**
THE MOMENTS YOU CHOSE GROWTH, CALM, COURAGE, OR CLARITY OVER CHAOS.	TANGIBLE MOVES YOU MADE — BIG OR SMALL — THAT PROVE YOU'RE BUILDING MOMENTUM.	WHEN SOMETHING FELT RIGHT, EASY, ALIGNED, OR JOYFULLY YOU.

WHAT NEEDS TO **SHIFT** ASAP?

HOW WAS MY **SLEEP LAST NIGHT**

(1) (2) (3) (4) (5) (6) (7) (8) (9) (10)

HOW **MOTIVATED** DO I FEEL TODAY

(1) (2) (3) (4) (5) (6) (7) (8) (9) (10)

WHERE IS MY **PHYSICAL ENERGY LEVEL**

(1) (2) (3) (4) (5) (6) (7) (8) (9) (10)

HOW IS MY **EMOTIONAL CAPACITY**

(1) (2) (3) (4) (5) (6) (7) (8) (9) (10)

SHITTY ——————————————— AWESOME

THREE THINGS I'M **GRATEFUL FOR:**

_____
_____
_____
_____
_____
_____
_____
_____

REFLECTION OF YESTERDAY

DID I DO THE THINGS I **COMMITED** TO DO? (Y) (N)

DID I DO SOMETHING FOR **MYSELF**? (joy, rest, movement, fun) (Y) (N)

DID I PROTECT MY **ENERGY** AND SET **CLEAR BOUNDARIES**? (Y) (N)

DID I **CELEBRATE** A SMALL WIN (or acknowledge progress) (Y) (N)

DID I CHECK IN WITH MY **VISION + GOALS** (even briefly)? (Y) (N)

DID I MAKE AT LEAST ONE **BOLD MOVE** OR **CEO DECISION**? (Y) (N)

DID I **STAY FOCUSED** ON MY GROWTH? (Y) (N)

IF I ANSWERED "NO" TO ANY **WHAT DO I SHIFT TODAY**?

_____
_____
_____
_____
_____

3 **ACTION STEPS** (COMMITMENTS) I WILL DO TODAY

THINGS YOU WILL COMMIT TO YOURSELF AND YOUR BUSINESS TO SUPPORT YOUR VISION

SOMETHING I NEED TO **REMIND MYSELF** OF TODAY _____

BUSINESS TO DO LIST:

PERSONAL TO DO LIST:

TOP PRIORITIES TODAY

_____

_____

_____

HOW MUCH **TIME** WILL I
DEDICATE TO MY BUSINESS
TODAY?

6 am

7 am

8 am

9 am

10 am

11 am

12 pm

1 pm

2 pm

3 pm

4 pm

5 pm

6 pm

7 pm

HOW WAS MY **SLEEP LAST NIGHT**

(1) (2) (3) (4) (5) (6) (7) (8) (9) (10)

HOW **MOTIVATED** DO I FEEL TODAY

(1) (2) (3) (4) (5) (6) (7) (8) (9) (10)

WHERE IS MY **PHYSICAL ENERGY LEVEL**

(1) (2) (3) (4) (5) (6) (7) (8) (9) (10)

HOW IS MY **EMOTIONAL CAPACITY**

(1) (2) (3) (4) (5) (6) (7) (8) (9) (10)

SHITTY ———————————————— AWESOME

THREE THINGS I'M **GRATEFUL FOR:**

_____
_____
_____
_____
_____
_____
_____
_____

REFLECTION OF YESTERDAY

DID I DO THE THINGS I **COMMITED** TO DO? (Y) (N)

DID I DO SOMETHING FOR **MYSELF**? (joy, rest, movement, fun) (Y) (N)

DID I PROTECT MY **ENERGY** AND SET **CLEAR BOUNDARIES**? (Y) (N)

DID I **CELEBRATE** A SMALL WIN (or acknowledge progress) (Y) (N)

DID I CHECK IN WITH MY **VISION + GOALS** (even briefly)? (Y) (N)

DID I MAKE AT LEAST ONE **BOLD MOVE** OR **CEO DECISION**? (Y) (N)

DID I **STAY FOCUSED** ON MY GROWTH? (Y) (N)

IF I ANSWERED "NO" TO ANY **WHAT DO I SHIFT TODAY**?

_____
_____
_____
_____
_____

3 **ACTION STEPS** (COMMITMENTS) I WILL DO TODAY
THINGS YOU WILL COMMIT TO YOURSELF AND YOUR BUSINESS TO SUPPORT YOUR VISION

SOMETHING I NEED TO **REMIND MYSELF** OF TODAY _____

BUSINESS TO DO LIST:

PERSONAL TO DO LIST:

TOP PRIORITIES TODAY

_____

_____

_____

_____

HOW MUCH **TIME** WILL I DEDICATE TO MY BUSINESS TODAY?

6 am

7 am

8 am

9 am

10 am

11 am

12 pm

1 pm

2 pm

3 pm

4 pm

5 pm

6 pm

7 pm

HOW WAS MY **SLEEP LAST NIGHT**

(1)(2)(3)(4)(5)(6)(7)(8)(9)(10)

HOW **MOTIVATED** DO I FEEL TODAY

(1)(2)(3)(4)(5)(6)(7)(8)(9)(10)

WHERE IS MY **PHYSICAL ENERGY LEVEL**

(1)(2)(3)(4)(5)(6)(7)(8)(9)(10)

HOW IS MY **EMOTIONAL CAPACITY**

(1)(2)(3)(4)(5)(6)(7)(8)(9)(10)

SHITTY ——————————————— AWESOME

THREE THINGS I'M
GRATEFUL FOR:

_____
_____
_____
_____
_____
_____
_____

REFLECTION OF YESTERDAY

DID I DO THE THINGS I **COMMITED** TO DO?   (Y)(N)

DID I DO SOMETHING FOR **MYSELF**? (joy, rest, movement, fun)   (Y)(N)

DID I PROTECT MY **ENERGY** AND SET **CLEAR BOUNDARIES**?   (Y)(N)

DID I **CELEBRATE** A SMALL WIN (or acknowledge progress)   (Y)(N)

DID I CHECK IN WITH MY **VISION + GOALS** (even briefly)?   (Y)(N)

DID I MAKE AT LEAST ONE **BOLD MOVE** OR **CEO DECISION**?   (Y)(N)

DID I **STAY FOCUSED** ON MY GROWTH?   (Y)(N)

IF I ANSWERED "NO" TO ANY
WHAT DO I SHIFT TODAY?

_____
_____
_____
_____
_____

3 ACTION STEPS (COMMITMENTS) I WILL DO TODAY

THINGS YOU WILL COMMIT TO YOURSELF AND YOUR BUSINESS TO SUPPORT YOUR VISION

SOMETHING I NEED TO **REMIND MYSELF** OF TODAY _____

_____

BUSINESS TO DO LIST:

PERSONAL TO DO LIST:

TOP PRIORITIES TODAY

_____

_____

_____

_____

HOW MUCH **TIME** WILL I DEDICATE TO MY BUSINESS TODAY?

6 am

7 am

8 am

9 am

10 am

11 am

12 pm

1 pm

2 pm

3 pm

4 pm

5 pm

6 pm

7 pm

HOW WAS MY **SLEEP LAST NIGHT**

(1) (2) (3) (4) (5) (6) (7) (8) (9) (10)

HOW **MOTIVATED** DO I FEEL TODAY

(1) (2) (3) (4) (5) (6) (7) (8) (9) (10)

WHERE IS MY **PHYSICAL ENERGY LEVEL**

(1) (2) (3) (4) (5) (6) (7) (8) (9) (10)

HOW IS MY **EMOTIONAL CAPACITY**

(1) (2) (3) (4) (5) (6) (7) (8) (9) (10)

SHITTY ———————————————————— AWESOME

THREE THINGS I'M **GRATEFUL FOR:**

_____
_____
_____
_____
_____
_____
_____

REFLECTION OF YESTERDAY

DID I DO THE THINGS I **COMMITED** TO DO? (Y) (N)

DID I DO SOMETHING FOR **MYSELF**? (joy, rest, movement, fun) (Y) (N)

DID I PROTECT MY **ENERGY** AND SET **CLEAR BOUNDARIES**? (Y) (N)

DID I **CELEBRATE** A SMALL WIN (or acknowledge progress) (Y) (N)

DID I CHECK IN WITH MY **VISION + GOALS** (even briefly)? (Y) (N)

DID I MAKE AT LEAST ONE **BOLD MOVE** OR **CEO DECISION**? (Y) (N)

DID I **STAY FOCUSED** ON MY GROWTH? (Y) (N)

IF I ANSWERED "NO" TO ANY **WHAT DO I SHIFT TODAY**?

_____
_____
_____
_____
_____

3 **ACTION STEPS** (COMMITMENTS) I WILL DO TODAY
THINGS YOU WILL COMMIT TO YOURSELF AND YOUR BUSINESS TO SUPPORT YOUR VISION

SOMETHING I NEED TO **REMIND MYSELF** OF TODAY _____

BUSINESS TO DO LIST:

PERSONAL TO DO LIST:

TOP PRIORITIES TODAY

_____

_____

_____

HOW MUCH **TIME** WILL I
DEDICATE TO MY BUSINESS
TODAY?

6 am

7 am

8 am

9 am

10 am

11 am

12 pm

1 pm

2 pm

3 pm

4 pm

5 pm

6 pm

7 pm

She's the STRATEGY
Unapologetically Authentic. Own That Damn Business

HOW WAS MY **SLEEP LAST NIGHT**

(1) (2) (3) (4) (5) (6) (7) (8) (9) (10)

HOW **MOTIVATED** DO I FEEL TODAY

(1) (2) (3) (4) (5) (6) (7) (8) (9) (10)

WHERE IS MY **PHYSICAL ENERGY LEVEL**

(1) (2) (3) (4) (5) (6) (7) (8) (9) (10)

HOW IS MY **EMOTIONAL CAPACITY**

(1) (2) (3) (4) (5) (6) (7) (8) (9) (10)

SHITTY ————————————————— AWESOME

THREE THINGS I'M **GRATEFUL FOR:**

_____
_____
_____
_____
_____
_____
_____

REFLECTION OF YESTERDAY

DID I DO THE THINGS I **COMMITED** TO DO? (Y) (N)

DID I DO SOMETHING FOR **MYSELF**? (joy, rest, movement, fun) (Y) (N)

DID I PROTECT MY **ENERGY** AND SET **CLEAR BOUNDARIES**? (Y) (N)

DID I **CELEBRATE** A SMALL WIN (or acknowledge progress) (Y) (N)

DID I CHECK IN WITH MY **VISION + GOALS** (even briefly)? (Y) (N)

DID I MAKE AT LEAST ONE **BOLD MOVE** OR **CEO DECISION**? (Y) (N)

DID I **STAY FOCUSED** ON MY GROWTH? (Y) (N)

IF I ANSWERED "NO" TO ANY **WHAT DO I SHIFT TODAY**?

_____
_____
_____
_____
_____

3 ACTION STEPS (COMMITMENTS) I WILL DO TODAY
THINGS YOU WILL COMMIT TO YOURSELF AND YOUR BUSINESS TO SUPPORT YOUR VISION

SOMETHING I NEED TO **REMIND MYSELF** OF TODAY _____

BUSINESS TO DO LIST:

PERSONAL TO DO LIST:

TOP PRIORITIES TODAY

_____

_____

_____

_____

HOW MUCH **TIME** WILL I DEDICATE TO MY BUSINESS TODAY?

6 am
_____

7 am
_____

8 am
_____

9 am
_____

10 am
_____

11 am
_____

12 pm
_____

1 pm
_____

2 pm
_____

3 pm
_____

4 pm
_____

5 pm
_____

6 pm
_____

7 pm
_____

HOW WAS MY **SLEEP LAST NIGHT**

(1) (2) (3) (4) (5) (6) (7) (8) (9) (10)

HOW **MOTIVATED** DO I FEEL TODAY

(1) (2) (3) (4) (5) (6) (7) (8) (9) (10)

WHERE IS MY **PHYSICAL ENERGY LEVEL**

(1) (2) (3) (4) (5) (6) (7) (8) (9) (10)

HOW IS MY **EMOTIONAL CAPACITY**

(1) (2) (3) (4) (5) (6) (7) (8) (9) (10)

SHITTY ——————————————— AWESOME

THREE THINGS I'M
GRATEFUL FOR:

_____
_____
_____
_____
_____
_____
_____

REFLECTION OF YESTERDAY

	Y / N
DID I DO THE THINGS I **COMMITED** TO DO?	(Y)(N)
DID I DO SOMETHING FOR **MYSELF**? (joy, rest, movement, fun)	(Y)(N)
DID I PROTECT MY **ENERGY** AND SET **CLEAR BOUNDARIES**?	(Y)(N)
DID I **CELEBRATE** A SMALL WIN (or acknowledge progress)	(Y)(N)
DID I CHECK IN WITH MY **VISION + GOALS** (even briefly)?	(Y)(N)
DID I MAKE AT LEAST ONE **BOLD MOVE** OR **CEO DECISION**?	(Y)(N)
DID I **STAY FOCUSED** ON MY GROWTH?	(Y)(N)

IF I ANSWERED "NO" TO ANY
WHAT DO I SHIFT TODAY?

_____
_____
_____
_____
_____
_____

3 **ACTION STEPS** (COMMITMENTS) I WILL DO TODAY
THINGS YOU WILL COMMIT TO YOURSELF AND YOUR BUSINESS TO SUPPORT YOUR VISION

SOMETHING I NEED TO **REMIND MYSELF** OF TODAY _____

BUSINESS TO DO LIST:

PERSONAL TO DO LIST:

TOP PRIORITIES TODAY

_____
_____
_____
_____

HOW MUCH **TIME** WILL I DEDICATE TO MY BUSINESS TODAY?

6 am
7 am
8 am
9 am
10 am
11 am
12 pm
1 pm
2 pm
3 pm
4 pm
5 pm
6 pm
7 pm

HOW WAS MY **SLEEP LAST NIGHT**

(1) (2) (3) (4) (5) (6) (7) (8) (9) (10)

HOW **MOTIVATED** DO I FEEL TODAY

(1) (2) (3) (4) (5) (6) (7) (8) (9) (10)

WHERE IS MY **PHYSICAL ENERGY LEVEL**

(1) (2) (3) (4) (5) (6) (7) (8) (9) (10)

HOW IS MY **EMOTIONAL CAPACITY**

(1) (2) (3) (4) (5) (6) (7) (8) (9) (10)

SHITTY ———————————————— AWESOME

THREE THINGS I'M **GRATEFUL FOR:**

_____
_____
_____
_____
_____
_____
_____

REFLECTION OF YESTERDAY

DID I DO THE THINGS I **COMMITED** TO DO? (Y) (N)

DID I DO SOMETHING FOR **MYSELF**? (joy, rest, movement, fun) (Y) (N)

DID I PROTECT MY **ENERGY** AND SET **CLEAR BOUNDARIES**? (Y) (N)

DID I **CELEBRATE** A SMALL WIN (or acknowledge progress) (Y) (N)

DID I CHECK IN WITH MY **VISION + GOALS** (even briefly)? (Y) (N)

DID I MAKE AT LEAST ONE **BOLD MOVE** OR **CEO DECISION**? (Y) (N)

DID I **STAY FOCUSED** ON MY GROWTH? (Y) (N)

IF I ANSWERED "NO" TO ANY **WHAT DO I SHIFT TODAY**?

_____
_____
_____
_____

3 **ACTION STEPS** (COMMITMENTS) I WILL DO TODAY
THINGS YOU WILL COMMIT TO YOURSELF AND YOUR BUSINESS TO SUPPORT YOUR VISION

SOMETHING I NEED TO **REMIND MYSELF** OF TODAY _____

BUSINESS TO DO LIST:

PERSONAL TO DO LIST:

TOP PRIORITIES TODAY

_____

_____

_____

_____

HOW MUCH **TIME** WILL I
DEDICATE TO MY BUSINESS
TODAY?

6 am

7 am

8 am

9 am

10 am

11 am

12 pm

1 pm

2 pm

3 pm

4 pm

5 pm

6 pm

7 pm

WEEKLY CHECK-IN

PERSONAL ENERGY & WELL-BEING
On a scale of 1–10, how would I rate...

MY OVERALL **ENERGY** THIS WEEK
(1) (2) (3) (4) (5) (6) (7) (8) (9) (10)

MY **EMOTIONAL CAPACITY** THIS WEEK
(1) (2) (3) (4) (5) (6) (7) (8) (9) (10)

MY **MOTIVATION + CLARITY** THIS WEEK
(1) (2) (3) (4) (5) (6) (7) (8) (9) (10)

SHITTY ———————————————— AWESOME

WHAT SUPPORTED MY WELL-BEING THIS WEEK?

_____

_____

WHAT DRAINED ME THAT I WANT TO SHIFT OR
ELIMINATE?

_____

_____

WHAT DID I DO JUST FOR ME THIS WEEK?

_____

_____

BUSINESS & LEADERSHIP REFLECTIONS

DID I **STAY FOCUSED** ON MY TOP PRIORITIES? (Y) (N)

DID I **LEAD** WITH CONFIDENCE, EVEN WHEN IT (Y) (N)
WAS HARD?

DID I **SHOW UP** FOR MY BRAND IN A WAY I'M (Y) (N)
PROUD OF?

DID I COMMUNICATE **CLEAR BOUNDARIES** (Y) (N)
AROUND MY TIME?

WHAT WORKED REALLY WELL IN MY
BUSINESS THIS WEEK?
_____

WHAT CHALLENGES CAME UP, AND WHAT
DID I LEARN FROM THEM?
_____

WHAT BOLD MOVE DID I MAKE (OR WISH I
HAD)?
_____

ALIGNMENT & INTENTION

AM I STILL MOVING TOWARD MY BIGGER
VISION — OR AM I JUST STAYING BUSY?

WHAT DO I NEED TO PAUSE, PIVOT, OR
RELEASE RIGHT NOW?

WHAT'S ONE THING I WANT TO RECOMMIT
TO NEXT WEEK?

NEXT WEEK'S FOCUS

ONE BOLD THING I'LL DO THIS WEEK

ONE BOUNDARY I'LL PROTECT

WEEKLY **GOAL PLANNER** LIKE A
DAMN BUSINESS BADASS

MY **WEEKLY** FOCUS
TOP 3 POWER GOALS FOR THIS WEEK - (WHAT ACTUALLY MOVES THE NEEDLE — NOT BUSY WORK.)

ENERGY + MINDSET FOCUS:

(ONE VIBE, MANTRA, OR ENERGY YOU'RE CHOOSING TO LEAD WITH THIS WEEK.) ....

CELEBRATE YOUR DAMN WINS:

INNER WINS **(MINDSET + ENERGY)** THE MOMENTS YOU CHOSE GROWTH, CALM, COURAGE, OR CLARITY OVER CHAOS.	**ACTION WINS** **(SH*T YOU ACTUALLY DID)** TANGIBLE MOVES YOU MADE — BIG OR SMALL — THAT PROVE YOU'RE BUILDING MOMENTUM.	**ALIGNMENT WINS** **(SOUL-LEVEL YES MOMENTS)** WHEN SOMETHING FELT RIGHT, EASY, ALIGNED, OR JOYFULLY YOU.

WHAT NEEDS TO **SHIFT** ASAP?

HOW WAS MY **SLEEP LAST NIGHT**

(1) (2) (3) (4) (5) (6) (7) (8) (9) (10)

HOW **MOTIVATED** DO I FEEL TODAY

(1) (2) (3) (4) (5) (6) (7) (8) (9) (10)

WHERE IS MY **PHYSICAL ENERGY LEVEL**

(1) (2) (3) (4) (5) (6) (7) (8) (9) (10)

HOW IS MY **EMOTIONAL CAPACITY**

(1) (2) (3) (4) (5) (6) (7) (8) (9) (10)

SHITTY ————————————— AWESOME

THREE THINGS I'M
GRATEFUL FOR:

_____

_____

_____

_____

_____

_____

REFLECTION OF YESTERDAY

DID I DO THE THINGS I **COMMITED** TO DO? (Y) (N)

DID I DO SOMETHING FOR **MYSELF**? (joy, rest, movement, fun) (Y) (N)

DID I PROTECT MY **ENERGY** AND SET **CLEAR BOUNDARIES**? (Y) (N)

DID I **CELEBRATE** A SMALL WIN (or acknowledge progress) (Y) (N)

DID I CHECK IN WITH MY **VISION + GOALS** (even briefly)? (Y) (N)

DID I MAKE AT LEAST ONE **BOLD MOVE** OR **CEO DECISION**? (Y) (N)

DID I **STAY FOCUSED** ON MY GROWTH? (Y) (N)

IF I ANSWERED "NO" TO ANY
WHAT DO I SHIFT TODAY?

_____

_____

_____

_____

3 **ACTION STEPS** (COMMITMENTS) I WILL DO TODAY
THINGS YOU WILL COMMIT TO YOURSELF AND YOUR BUSINESS TO SUPPORT YOUR VISION

SOMETHING I NEED TO **REMIND MYSELF** OF TODAY _____

BUSINESS TO DO LIST:

PERSONAL TO DO LIST:

TOP PRIORITIES TODAY

_____

_____

_____

HOW MUCH **TIME** WILL I DEDICATE TO MY BUSINESS TODAY?

6 am

7 am

8 am

9 am

10 am

11 am

12 pm

1 pm

2 pm

3 pm

4 pm

5 pm

6 pm

7 pm

HOW WAS MY **SLEEP LAST NIGHT**

(1) (2) (3) (4) (5) (6) (7) (8) (9) (10)

HOW **MOTIVATED** DO I FEEL TODAY

(1) (2) (3) (4) (5) (6) (7) (8) (9) (10)

WHERE IS MY **PHYSICAL ENERGY LEVEL**

(1) (2) (3) (4) (5) (6) (7) (8) (9) (10)

HOW IS MY **EMOTIONAL CAPACITY**

(1) (2) (3) (4) (5) (6) (7) (8) (9) (10)

SHITTY ———————————————— AWESOME

THREE THINGS I'M
GRATEFUL FOR:

_____
_____
_____
_____
_____
_____
_____

REFLECTION OF YESTERDAY

DID I DO THE THINGS I **COMMITED** TO DO?   (Y)(N)

DID I DO SOMETHING FOR **MYSELF**? (joy, rest, movement, fun)   (Y)(N)

DID I PROTECT MY **ENERGY** AND SET **CLEAR BOUNDARIES**?   (Y)(N)

DID I **CELEBRATE** A SMALL WIN (or acknowledge progress)   (Y)(N)

DID I CHECK IN WITH MY **VISION + GOALS** (even briefly)?   (Y)(N)

DID I MAKE AT LEAST ONE **BOLD MOVE** OR **CEO DECISION**?   (Y)(N)

DID I **STAY FOCUSED** ON MY GROWTH?   (Y)(N)

IF I ANSWERED "NO" TO ANY
WHAT DO I SHIFT TODAY?

_____
_____
_____
_____

3 **ACTION STEPS** (COMMITMENTS) I WILL DO TODAY
THINGS YOU WILL COMMIT TO YOURSELF AND YOUR BUSINESS TO SUPPORT YOUR VISION

SOMETHING I NEED TO **REMIND MYSELF** OF TODAY _____

BUSINESS TO DO LIST:

PERSONAL TO DO LIST:

TOP PRIORITIES TODAY

HOW MUCH **TIME** WILL I DEDICATE TO MY BUSINESS TODAY?

6 am

7 am

8 am

9 am

10 am

11 am

12 pm

1 pm

2 pm

3 pm

4 pm

5 pm

6 pm

7 pm

HOW WAS MY **SLEEP LAST NIGHT**

1 2 3 4 5 6 7 8 9 10

HOW **MOTIVATED** DO I FEEL TODAY

1 2 3 4 5 6 7 8 9 10

WHERE IS MY **PHYSICAL ENERGY LEVEL**

1 2 3 4 5 6 7 8 9 10

HOW IS MY **EMOTIONAL CAPACITY**

1 2 3 4 5 6 7 8 9 10

SHITTY ———————————————————— AWESOME

THREE THINGS I'M **GRATEFUL FOR:**

_____
_____
_____
_____
_____
_____
_____

REFLECTION OF YESTERDAY

DID I DO THE THINGS I **COMMITED** TO DO?   Y N

DID I DO SOMETHING FOR **MYSELF**? (joy, rest, movement, fun)   Y N

DID I PROTECT MY **ENERGY** AND SET **CLEAR BOUNDARIES**?   Y N

DID I **CELEBRATE** A SMALL WIN (or acknowledge progress)   Y N

DID I CHECK IN WITH MY **VISION + GOALS** (even briefly)?   Y N

DID I MAKE AT LEAST ONE **BOLD MOVE** OR **CEO DECISION**?   Y N

DID I **STAY FOCUSED** ON MY GROWTH?   Y N

IF I ANSWERED "NO" TO ANY **WHAT DO I SHIFT TODAY**?

_____
_____
_____
_____
_____

3 ACTION STEPS (COMMITMENTS) I WILL DO TODAY
THINGS YOU WILL COMMIT TO YOURSELF AND YOUR BUSINESS TO SUPPORT YOUR VISION

SOMETHING I NEED TO **REMIND MYSELF** OF TODAY _____

BUSINESS TO DO LIST:

PERSONAL TO DO LIST:

TOP PRIORITIES TODAY

_____

_____

_____

HOW MUCH **TIME** WILL I DEDICATE TO MY BUSINESS TODAY?

6 am

7 am

8 am

9 am

10 am

11 am

12 pm

1 pm

2 pm

3 pm

4 pm

5 pm

6 pm

7 pm

She's the STRATEGY
Unapologetically Authentic. Own That Damn Business.

HOW WAS MY **SLEEP LAST NIGHT**

1 2 3 4 5 6 7 8 9 10

HOW **MOTIVATED** DO I FEEL TODAY

1 2 3 4 5 6 7 8 9 10

WHERE IS MY **PHYSICAL ENERGY LEVEL**

1 2 3 4 5 6 7 8 9 10

HOW IS MY **EMOTIONAL CAPACITY**

1 2 3 4 5 6 7 8 9 10

SHITTY ——————————————— AWESOME

THREE THINGS I'M **GRATEFUL FOR:**

_____
_____
_____
_____
_____
_____

REFLECTION OF YESTERDAY

DID I DO THE THINGS I **COMMITED** TO DO? Y N

DID I DO SOMETHING FOR **MYSELF**? (joy, rest, movement, fun) Y N

DID I PROTECT MY **ENERGY** AND SET **CLEAR BOUNDARIES**? Y N

DID I **CELEBRATE** A SMALL WIN (or acknowledge progress) Y N

DID I CHECK IN WITH MY **VISION + GOALS** (even briefly)? Y N

DID I MAKE AT LEAST ONE **BOLD MOVE** OR **CEO DECISION**? Y N

DID I **STAY FOCUSED** ON MY GROWTH? Y N

IF I ANSWERED "NO" TO ANY
WHAT DO I SHIFT TODAY?

_____
_____
_____
_____
_____

3 ACTION STEPS (COMMITMENTS) I WILL DO TODAY
THINGS YOU WILL COMMIT TO YOURSELF AND YOUR BUSINESS TO SUPPORT YOUR VISION

SOMETHING I NEED TO **REMIND MYSELF** OF TODAY _____

BUSINESS TO DO LIST:

PERSONAL TO DO LIST:

TOP PRIORITIES TODAY

_____

_____

_____

HOW MUCH **TIME** WILL I
DEDICATE TO MY BUSINESS
TODAY?

6 am

7 am

8 am

9 am

10 am

11 am

12 pm

1 pm

2 pm

3 pm

4 pm

5 pm

6 pm

7 pm

HOW WAS MY **SLEEP LAST NIGHT**

① ② ③ ④ ⑤ ⑥ ⑦ ⑧ ⑨ ⑩

HOW **MOTIVATED** DO I FEEL TODAY

① ② ③ ④ ⑤ ⑥ ⑦ ⑧ ⑨ ⑩

WHERE IS MY **PHYSICAL ENERGY LEVEL**

① ② ③ ④ ⑤ ⑥ ⑦ ⑧ ⑨ ⑩

HOW IS MY **EMOTIONAL CAPACITY**

① ② ③ ④ ⑤ ⑥ ⑦ ⑧ ⑨ ⑩

SHITTY ———————————————— AWESOME

THREE THINGS I'M **GRATEFUL FOR:**

_____
_____
_____
_____
_____
_____
_____
_____

REFLECTION OF YESTERDAY

DID I DO THE THINGS I **COMMITED** TO DO?   Ⓨ Ⓝ

DID I DO SOMETHING FOR **MYSELF**? (joy, rest, movement, fun)   Ⓨ Ⓝ

DID I PROTECT MY **ENERGY** AND SET **CLEAR BOUNDARIES**?   Ⓨ Ⓝ

DID I **CELEBRATE** A SMALL WIN (or acknowledge progress)   Ⓨ Ⓝ

DID I CHECK IN WITH MY **VISION + GOALS** (even briefly)?   Ⓨ Ⓝ

DID I MAKE AT LEAST ONE **BOLD MOVE** OR **CEO DECISION**?   Ⓨ Ⓝ

DID I **STAY FOCUSED** ON MY GROWTH?   Ⓨ Ⓝ

IF I ANSWERED "NO" TO ANY **WHAT DO I SHIFT TODAY**?

_____
_____
_____
_____
_____

---

3 ACTION STEPS (COMMITMENTS) I WILL DO TODAY

THINGS YOU WILL COMMIT TO YOURSELF AND YOUR BUSINESS TO SUPPORT YOUR VISION

SOMETHING I NEED TO **REMIND MYSELF** OF TODAY _____

_____

BUSINESS TO DO LIST:

PERSONAL TO DO LIST:

TOP PRIORITIES TODAY

_____

_____

_____

_____

HOW MUCH **TIME** WILL I DEDICATE TO MY BUSINESS TODAY?

6 am

7 am

8 am

9 am

10 am

11 am

12 pm

1 pm

2 pm

3 pm

4 pm

5 pm

6 pm

7 pm

HOW WAS MY **SLEEP LAST NIGHT**

① ② ③ ④ ⑤ ⑥ ⑦ ⑧ ⑨ ⑩

HOW **MOTIVATED** DO I FEEL TODAY

① ② ③ ④ ⑤ ⑥ ⑦ ⑧ ⑨ ⑩

WHERE IS MY **PHYSICAL ENERGY LEVEL**

① ② ③ ④ ⑤ ⑥ ⑦ ⑧ ⑨ ⑩

HOW IS MY **EMOTIONAL CAPACITY**

① ② ③ ④ ⑤ ⑥ ⑦ ⑧ ⑨ ⑩

SHITTY ———————————————— AWESOME

THREE THINGS I'M **GRATEFUL FOR:**

_____
_____
_____
_____
_____
_____

REFLECTION OF YESTERDAY

DID I DO THE THINGS I **COMMITED** TO DO?	Y	N
DID I DO SOMETHING FOR **MYSELF**? (joy, rest, movement, fun)	Y	N
DID I PROTECT MY **ENERGY** AND SET **CLEAR BOUNDARIES**?	Y	N
DID I **CELEBRATE** A SMALL WIN (or acknowledge progress)	Y	N
DID I CHECK IN WITH MY **VISION + GOALS** (even briefly)?	Y	N
DID I MAKE AT LEAST ONE **BOLD MOVE** OR **CEO DECISION**?	Y	N
DID I **STAY FOCUSED** ON MY GROWTH?	Y	N

IF I ANSWERED "NO" TO ANY
WHAT DO I SHIFT TODAY?

_____
_____
_____
_____
_____

3 ACTION STEPS (COMMITMENTS) I WILL DO TODAY
THINGS YOU WILL COMMIT TO YOURSELF AND YOUR BUSINESS TO SUPPORT YOUR VISION

SOMETHING I NEED TO **REMIND MYSELF** OF TODAY _____

BUSINESS TO DO LIST:

PERSONAL TO DO LIST:

TOP PRIORITIES TODAY

_____

_____

_____

HOW MUCH **TIME** WILL I DEDICATE TO MY BUSINESS TODAY?

6 am

7 am

8 am

9 am

10 am

11 am

12 pm

1 pm

2 pm

3 pm

4 pm

5 pm

6 pm

7 pm

HOW WAS MY **SLEEP LAST NIGHT**

① ② ③ ④ ⑤ ⑥ ⑦ ⑧ ⑨ ⑩

HOW **MOTIVATED** DO I FEEL TODAY

① ② ③ ④ ⑤ ⑥ ⑦ ⑧ ⑨ ⑩

WHERE IS MY **PHYSICAL ENERGY LEVEL**

① ② ③ ④ ⑤ ⑥ ⑦ ⑧ ⑨ ⑩

HOW IS MY **EMOTIONAL CAPACITY**

① ② ③ ④ ⑤ ⑥ ⑦ ⑧ ⑨ ⑩

SHITTY ——————————————————— AWESOME

THREE THINGS I'M **GRATEFUL FOR:**

_____
_____
_____
_____
_____
_____
_____

REFLECTION OF YESTERDAY

DID I DO THE THINGS I **COMMITED** TO DO? Ⓨ Ⓝ

DID I DO SOMETHING FOR **MYSELF**? (joy, rest, movement, fun) Ⓨ Ⓝ

DID I PROTECT MY **ENERGY** AND SET **CLEAR BOUNDARIES**? Ⓨ Ⓝ

DID I **CELEBRATE** A SMALL WIN (or acknowledge progress) Ⓨ Ⓝ

DID I CHECK IN WITH MY **VISION + GOALS** (even briefly)? Ⓨ Ⓝ

DID I MAKE AT LEAST ONE **BOLD MOVE** OR **CEO DECISION**? Ⓨ Ⓝ

DID I **STAY FOCUSED** ON MY GROWTH? Ⓨ Ⓝ

IF I ANSWERED "NO" TO ANY **WHAT DO I SHIFT TODAY**?

_____
_____
_____
_____
_____

3 **ACTION STEPS** (COMMITMENTS) I WILL DO TODAY

THINGS YOU WILL COMMIT TO YOURSELF AND YOUR BUSINESS TO SUPPORT YOUR VISION

SOMETHING I NEED TO **REMIND MYSELF** OF TODAY _____

BUSINESS TO DO LIST:

PERSONAL TO DO LIST:

TOP PRIORITIES TODAY

_____

_____

_____

_____

HOW MUCH **TIME** WILL I
DEDICATE TO MY BUSINESS
TODAY?

6 am

7 am

8 am

9 am

10 am

11 am

12 pm

1 pm

2 pm

3 pm

4 pm

5 pm

6 pm

7 pm

MONTHLY CHECK-IN
A MOMENT TO ZOOM OUT, REALIGN, AND POWER UP.

MONTHLY WINS

MY **PROUDEST** MOMENT

A MILESTONE I **REACHED** (BIG OR SMALL):

A CHALLENGE I **OVERCAME**

BY THE NUMBERS

CLIENTS SERVED: _____

REVENUE/INCOME: _____

OFFERS PROMOTED/LAUNCHED: _____

PERSONAL REFLECTION

I FELT LIKE THE CEO OF MY LIFE ⓨ ⓝ

I TOOK CARE OF MYSELF CONSISTENTLY ⓨ ⓝ

I FELT ALIGNED WITH MY BUSINESS VISION: ⓨ ⓝ

WHAT DID I LEARN ABOUT MYSELF THIS MONTH? _____

_____

WHAT DO I WANT TO CELEBRATE MORE OFTEN? _____

_____

WHAT BELIEF OR HABIT NEEDS TO SHIFT NEXT MONTH? _____

_____

RESET + RECOMMIT

WHAT WILL I TAKE WITH ME INTO NEXT MONTH?	WHAT WILL I LEAVE BEHIND WITH?	WHAT DO I WANT TO EXPERIENCE MORE OF?

MY **FOCUS THEME** FOR **NEXT MONTH**: _____

MONTHLY **GOAL PLANNER** LIKE A
DAMN BUSINESS BADASS

MY **MONTHLY** FOCUS

MONTH: _____

WHAT SPECIFIC OUTCOME DO I WANT TO CREATE BY THE END OF THIS MONTH?

MY **MEASURABLE** GOAL
(CLIENT COUNT, REVENUE TARGET, AUDIENCE GROWTH, ETC.) _____

_____

MY SUPPORT SYSTEM	**MY SELF-CARE STRATEGY**	**VISION BUILDER**
WHAT SUPPORT, TOOLS, OR PEOPLE DO I NEED TO HELP ME MOVE FORWARD?	WHAT WILL BALANCE, REST, OR JOY LOOK LIKE THIS MONTH?	WHO AM I BECOMING IN THIS BUSINESS?

QUARTER: **Q1 / Q2 / Q3 / Q4** (CIRCLE ONE)

YEAR: _____

IF I FULLY TRUSTED MYSELF, WHAT WOULD I CREATE OR LAUNCH THIS QUARTER? _____

_____

WHAT DOES SUCCESS LOOK AND FEEL LIKE TO ME (NOT SOCIETY'S VERSION)? _____

_____

WHAT DO I WANT TO BE KNOWN FOR BY THE END OF THIS QUARTER?

_____

She's the
STRATEGY
Unapologetically Authentic. Own That Damn Business.

HOW WAS MY **SLEEP LAST NIGHT**

(1) (2) (3) (4) (5) (6) (7) (8) (9) (10)

HOW **MOTIVATED** DO I FEEL TODAY

(1) (2) (3) (4) (5) (6) (7) (8) (9) (10)

WHERE IS MY **PHYSICAL ENERGY LEVEL**

(1) (2) (3) (4) (5) (6) (7) (8) (9) (10)

HOW IS MY **EMOTIONAL CAPACITY**

(1) (2) (3) (4) (5) (6) (7) (8) (9) (10)

SHITTY ——————————————————— AWESOME

THREE THINGS I'M **GRATEFUL FOR:**

_____
_____
_____
_____
_____
_____
_____
_____

REFLECTION OF YESTERDAY

	Y	N
DID I DO THE THINGS I **COMMITED** TO DO?	Y	N
DID I DO SOMETHING FOR **MYSELF**? (joy, rest, movement, fun)	Y	N
DID I PROTECT MY **ENERGY** AND SET **CLEAR BOUNDARIES**?	Y	N
DID I **CELEBRATE** A SMALL WIN (or acknowledge progress)	Y	N
DID I CHECK IN WITH MY **VISION + GOALS** (even briefly)?	Y	N
DID I MAKE AT LEAST ONE **BOLD MOVE** OR **CEO DECISION**?	Y	N
DID I **STAY FOCUSED** ON MY GROWTH?	Y	N

IF I ANSWERED "NO" TO ANY
WHAT DO I SHIFT TODAY?

_____
_____
_____
_____
_____

3 ACTION STEPS (COMMITMENTS) I WILL DO TODAY
THINGS YOU WILL COMMIT TO YOURSELF AND YOUR BUSINESS TO SUPPORT YOUR VISION

SOMETHING I NEED TO **REMIND MYSELF** OF TODAY _____

BUSINESS TO DO LIST:

PERSONAL TO DO LIST:

TOP PRIORITIES TODAY

_____

_____

_____

HOW MUCH **TIME** WILL I
DEDICATE TO MY BUSINESS
TODAY?

6 am

7 am

8 am

9 am

10 am

11 am

12 pm

1 pm

2 pm

3 pm

4 pm

5 pm

6 pm

7 pm

HOW WAS MY **SLEEP LAST NIGHT**

① ② ③ ④ ⑤ ⑥ ⑦ ⑧ ⑨ ⑩

HOW **MOTIVATED** DO I FEEL TODAY

① ② ③ ④ ⑤ ⑥ ⑦ ⑧ ⑨ ⑩

WHERE IS MY **PHYSICAL ENERGY LEVEL**

① ② ③ ④ ⑤ ⑥ ⑦ ⑧ ⑨ ⑩

HOW IS MY **EMOTIONAL CAPACITY**

① ② ③ ④ ⑤ ⑥ ⑦ ⑧ ⑨ ⑩

SHITTY ————————————————— AWESOME

THREE THINGS I'M **GRATEFUL FOR:**

_____
_____
_____
_____
_____
_____
_____

REFLECTION OF YESTERDAY

DID I DO THE THINGS I **COMMITED** TO DO? Ⓨ Ⓝ

DID I DO SOMETHING FOR **MYSELF**? (joy, rest, movement, fun) Ⓨ Ⓝ

DID I PROTECT MY **ENERGY** AND SET **CLEAR BOUNDARIES**? Ⓨ Ⓝ

DID I **CELEBRATE** A SMALL WIN (or acknowledge progress) Ⓨ Ⓝ

DID I CHECK IN WITH MY **VISION + GOALS** (even briefly)? Ⓨ Ⓝ

DID I MAKE AT LEAST ONE **BOLD MOVE** OR **CEO DECISION**? Ⓨ Ⓝ

DID I **STAY FOCUSED** ON MY GROWTH? Ⓨ Ⓝ

IF I ANSWERED "NO" TO ANY **WHAT DO I SHIFT TODAY**?

_____
_____
_____
_____
_____

3 ACTION STEPS (COMMITMENTS) I WILL DO TODAY
THINGS YOU WILL COMMIT TO YOURSELF AND YOUR BUSINESS TO SUPPORT YOUR VISION

SOMETHING I NEED TO **REMIND MYSELF** OF TODAY _____

BUSINESS TO DO LIST:

PERSONAL TO DO LIST:

TOP PRIORITIES TODAY

_____

_____

_____

HOW MUCH **TIME** WILL I DEDICATE TO MY BUSINESS TODAY?

6 am

7 am

8 am

9 am

10 am

11 am

12 pm

1 pm

2 pm

3 pm

4 pm

5 pm

6 pm

7 pm

HOW WAS MY **SLEEP LAST NIGHT**

① ② ③ ④ ⑤ ⑥ ⑦ ⑧ ⑨ ⑩

HOW **MOTIVATED** DO I FEEL TODAY

① ② ③ ④ ⑤ ⑥ ⑦ ⑧ ⑨ ⑩

WHERE IS MY **PHYSICAL ENERGY LEVEL**

① ② ③ ④ ⑤ ⑥ ⑦ ⑧ ⑨ ⑩

HOW IS MY **EMOTIONAL CAPACITY**

① ② ③ ④ ⑤ ⑥ ⑦ ⑧ ⑨ ⑩

SHITTY ——————————————— AWESOME

THREE THINGS I'M **GRATEFUL FOR:**

_____
_____
_____
_____
_____
_____
_____

REFLECTION OF YESTERDAY

DID I DO THE THINGS I **COMMITED** TO DO? Ⓨ Ⓝ

DID I DO SOMETHING FOR **MYSELF**? (joy, rest, movement, fun) Ⓨ Ⓝ

DID I PROTECT MY **ENERGY** AND SET **CLEAR BOUNDARIES**? Ⓨ Ⓝ

DID I **CELEBRATE** A SMALL WIN (or acknowledge progress) Ⓨ Ⓝ

DID I CHECK IN WITH MY **VISION + GOALS** (even briefly)? Ⓨ Ⓝ

DID I MAKE AT LEAST ONE **BOLD MOVE** OR **CEO DECISION**? Ⓨ Ⓝ

DID I **STAY FOCUSED** ON MY GROWTH? Ⓨ Ⓝ

IF I ANSWERED "NO" TO ANY **WHAT DO I SHIFT TODAY**?

_____
_____
_____
_____
_____

3 **ACTION STEPS** (COMMITMENTS) I WILL DO TODAY
THINGS YOU WILL COMMIT TO YOURSELF AND YOUR BUSINESS TO SUPPORT YOUR VISION

SOMETHING I NEED TO **REMIND MYSELF** OF TODAY _____

BUSINESS TO DO LIST:

PERSONAL TO DO LIST:

TOP PRIORITIES TODAY

_____

_____

_____

HOW MUCH **TIME** WILL I DEDICATE TO MY BUSINESS TODAY?

6 am

7 am

8 am

9 am

10 am

11 am

12 pm

1 pm

2 pm

3 pm

4 pm

5 pm

6 pm

7 pm

She's the STRATEGY
Unapologetically Authentic. Own That Damn Business

JAN FEB MAR APR MAY JUN JUL AUG SEP OCT NOV DEC 20___
1 2 3 4 5 6 7 8 9 10 11 12 13 14 15 16 17 18 19 20 21 22 23 24 25 26 27 28 29 30 31

HOW WAS MY **SLEEP LAST NIGHT**

1 2 3 4 5 6 7 8 9 10

HOW **MOTIVATED** DO I FEEL TODAY

1 2 3 4 5 6 7 8 9 10

WHERE IS MY **PHYSICAL ENERGY LEVEL**

1 2 3 4 5 6 7 8 9 10

HOW IS MY **EMOTIONAL CAPACITY**

1 2 3 4 5 6 7 8 9 10

SHITTY ————————————————— AWESOME

THREE THINGS I'M **GRATEFUL FOR:**

_____
_____
_____
_____
_____
_____
_____

REFLECTION OF YESTERDAY

DID I DO THE THINGS I **COMMITED** TO DO?   Y N

DID I DO SOMETHING FOR **MYSELF**? (joy, rest, movement, fun)   Y N

DID I PROTECT MY **ENERGY** AND SET **CLEAR BOUNDARIES**?   Y N

DID I **CELEBRATE** A SMALL WIN (or acknowledge progress)   Y N

DID I CHECK IN WITH MY **VISION + GOALS** (even briefly)?   Y N

DID I MAKE AT LEAST ONE **BOLD MOVE** OR **CEO DECISION**?   Y N

DID I **STAY FOCUSED** ON MY GROWTH?   Y N

IF I ANSWERED "NO" TO ANY **WHAT DO I SHIFT TODAY**?

_____
_____
_____
_____
_____

3 ACTION STEPS (COMMITMENTS) I WILL DO TODAY
THINGS YOU WILL COMMIT TO YOURSELF AND YOUR BUSINESS TO SUPPORT YOUR VISION

SOMETHING I NEED TO **REMIND MYSELF** OF TODAY _____

BUSINESS TO DO LIST:

PERSONAL TO DO LIST:

TOP PRIORITIES TODAY

_____

_____

_____

_____

HOW MUCH **TIME** WILL I DEDICATE TO MY BUSINESS TODAY?

6 am

7 am

8 am

9 am

10 am

11 am

12 pm

1 pm

2 pm

3 pm

4 pm

5 pm

6 pm

7 pm

HOW WAS MY **SLEEP LAST NIGHT**

(1) (2) (3) (4) (5) (6) (7) (8) (9) (10)

HOW **MOTIVATED** DO I FEEL TODAY

(1) (2) (3) (4) (5) (6) (7) (8) (9) (10)

WHERE IS MY **PHYSICAL ENERGY LEVEL**

(1) (2) (3) (4) (5) (6) (7) (8) (9) (10)

HOW IS MY **EMOTIONAL CAPACITY**

(1) (2) (3) (4) (5) (6) (7) (8) (9) (10)

SHITTY ——————————————————— AWESOME

THREE THINGS I'M **GRATEFUL FOR:**

_____
_____
_____
_____
_____
_____
_____

REFLECTION OF YESTERDAY

DID I DO THE THINGS I **COMMITED** TO DO? (Y) (N)

DID I DO SOMETHING FOR **MYSELF**? (joy, rest, movement, fun) (Y) (N)

DID I PROTECT MY **ENERGY** AND SET **CLEAR BOUNDARIES**? (Y) (N)

DID I **CELEBRATE** A SMALL WIN (or acknowledge progress) (Y) (N)

DID I CHECK IN WITH MY **VISION + GOALS** (even briefly)? (Y) (N)

DID I MAKE AT LEAST ONE **BOLD MOVE** OR **CEO DECISION**? (Y) (N)

DID I **STAY FOCUSED** ON MY GROWTH? (Y) (N)

IF I ANSWERED "NO" TO ANY **WHAT DO I SHIFT TODAY**?

_____
_____
_____
_____
_____

3 **ACTION STEPS** (COMMITMENTS) I WILL DO TODAY
THINGS YOU WILL COMMIT TO YOURSELF AND YOUR BUSINESS TO SUPPORT YOUR VISION

SOMETHING I NEED TO **REMIND MYSELF** OF TODAY _____

BUSINESS TO DO LIST:

PERSONAL TO DO LIST:

TOP PRIORITIES TODAY

_____

_____

_____

_____

HOW MUCH **TIME** WILL I DEDICATE TO MY BUSINESS TODAY?

6 am

7 am

8 am

9 am

10 am

11 am

12 pm

1 pm

2 pm

3 pm

4 pm

5 pm

6 pm

7 pm

HOW WAS MY **SLEEP LAST NIGHT**

① ② ③ ④ ⑤ ⑥ ⑦ ⑧ ⑨ ⑩

HOW **MOTIVATED** DO I FEEL TODAY

① ② ③ ④ ⑤ ⑥ ⑦ ⑧ ⑨ ⑩

WHERE IS MY **PHYSICAL ENERGY LEVEL**

① ② ③ ④ ⑤ ⑥ ⑦ ⑧ ⑨ ⑩

HOW IS MY **EMOTIONAL CAPACITY**

① ② ③ ④ ⑤ ⑥ ⑦ ⑧ ⑨ ⑩

SHITTY ———————————————— AWESOME

THREE THINGS I'M **GRATEFUL FOR:**

_____
_____
_____
_____
_____
_____

REFLECTION OF YESTERDAY

	Y	N
DID I DO THE THINGS I **COMMITED** TO DO?	Y	N
DID I DO SOMETHING FOR **MYSELF**? (joy, rest, movement, fun)	Y	N
DID I PROTECT MY **ENERGY** AND SET **CLEAR BOUNDARIES**?	Y	N
DID I **CELEBRATE** A SMALL WIN (or acknowledge progress)	Y	N
DID I CHECK IN WITH MY **VISION + GOALS** (even briefly)?	Y	N
DID I MAKE AT LEAST ONE **BOLD MOVE** OR **CEO DECISION**?	Y	N
DID I **STAY FOCUSED** ON MY GROWTH?	Y	N

IF I ANSWERED "NO" TO ANY **WHAT DO I SHIFT TODAY**?

_____
_____
_____
_____
_____

3 ACTION STEPS (COMMITMENTS) I WILL DO TODAY
THINGS YOU WILL COMMIT TO YOURSELF AND YOUR BUSINESS TO SUPPORT YOUR VISION

SOMETHING I NEED TO **REMIND MYSELF** OF TODAY _____

BUSINESS TO DO LIST:

PERSONAL TO DO LIST:

TOP PRIORITIES TODAY

_____
_____
_____

HOW MUCH **TIME** WILL I
DEDICATE TO MY BUSINESS
TODAY?

6 am

7 am

8 am

9 am

10 am

11 am

12 pm

1 pm

2 pm

3 pm

4 pm

5 pm

6 pm

7 pm

HOW WAS MY **SLEEP LAST NIGHT**

(1) (2) (3) (4) (5) (6) (7) (8) (9) (10)

HOW **MOTIVATED** DO I FEEL TODAY

(1) (2) (3) (4) (5) (6) (7) (8) (9) (10)

WHERE IS MY **PHYSICAL ENERGY LEVEL**

(1) (2) (3) (4) (5) (6) (7) (8) (9) (10)

HOW IS MY **EMOTIONAL CAPACITY**

(1) (2) (3) (4) (5) (6) (7) (8) (9) (10)

SHITTY ———————————————————— AWESOME

THREE THINGS I'M **GRATEFUL FOR:**

_____
_____
_____
_____
_____
_____
_____

REFLECTION OF YESTERDAY

DID I DO THE THINGS I **COMMITED** TO DO?   (Y) (N)

DID I DO SOMETHING FOR **MYSELF**? (joy, rest, movement, fun)   (Y) (N)

DID I PROTECT MY **ENERGY** AND SET **CLEAR BOUNDARIES**?   (Y) (N)

DID I **CELEBRATE** A SMALL WIN (or acknowledge progress)   (Y) (N)

DID I CHECK IN WITH MY **VISION + GOALS** (even briefly)?   (Y) (N)

DID I MAKE AT LEAST ONE **BOLD MOVE** OR **CEO DECISION**?   (Y) (N)

DID I **STAY FOCUSED** ON MY GROWTH?   (Y) (N)

IF I ANSWERED "NO" TO ANY **WHAT DO I SHIFT TODAY**?

_____
_____
_____
_____
_____

3 **ACTION STEPS** (COMMITMENTS) I WILL DO TODAY

THINGS YOU WILL COMMIT TO YOURSELF AND YOUR BUSINESS TO SUPPORT YOUR VISION

SOMETHING I NEED TO **REMIND MYSELF** OF TODAY _____

BUSINESS TO DO LIST:

PERSONAL TO DO LIST:

TOP PRIORITIES TODAY

_____

_____

_____

HOW MUCH **TIME** WILL I DEDICATE TO MY BUSINESS TODAY?

6 am

7 am

8 am

9 am

10 am

11 am

12 pm

1 pm

2 pm

3 pm

4 pm

5 pm

6 pm

7 pm

WEEKLY CHECK-IN

PERSONAL ENERGY & WELL-BEING
On a scale of 1–10, how would I rate...

MY OVERALL **ENERGY** THIS WEEK

(1) (2) (3) (4) (5) (6) (7) (8) (9) (10)

MY **EMOTIONAL CAPACITY** THIS WEEK

(1) (2) (3) (4) (5) (6) (7) (8) (9) (10)

MY **MOTIVATION + CLARITY** THIS WEEK

(1) (2) (3) (4) (5) (6) (7) (8) (9) (10)

SHITTY ——————————————— AWESOME

WHAT SUPPORTED MY WELL-BEING THIS WEEK?

_____

_____

WHAT DRAINED ME THAT I WANT TO SHIFT OR ELIMINATE?

_____

_____

WHAT DID I DO JUST FOR ME THIS WEEK?

_____

_____

BUSINESS & LEADERSHIP REFLECTIONS

DID I **STAY FOCUSED** ON MY TOP PRIORITIES? (Y) (N)

DID I **LEAD** WITH CONFIDENCE, EVEN WHEN IT WAS HARD? (Y) (N)

DID I **SHOW UP** FOR MY BRAND IN A WAY I'M PROUD OF? (Y) (N)

DID I COMMUNICATE **CLEAR BOUNDARIES** AROUND MY TIME? (Y) (N)

WHAT WORKED REALLY WELL IN MY BUSINESS THIS WEEK?

WHAT CHALLENGES CAME UP, AND WHAT DID I LEARN FROM THEM?

WHAT BOLD MOVE DID I MAKE (OR WISH I HAD)?

ALIGNMENT & INTENTION

AM I STILL MOVING TOWARD MY BIGGER VISION — OR AM I JUST STAYING BUSY?

WHAT DO I NEED TO PAUSE, PIVOT, OR RELEASE RIGHT NOW?

WHAT'S ONE THING I WANT TO RECOMMIT TO NEXT WEEK?

NEXT WEEK'S FOCUS

ONE BOLD THING I'LL DO THIS WEEK

ONE BOUNDARY I'LL PROTECT

WEEKLY **GOAL PLANNER** LIKE A
DAMN BUSINESS BADASS

MY **WEEKLY** FOCUS
TOP 3 POWER GOALS FOR THIS WEEK - (WHAT ACTUALLY MOVES THE NEEDLE — NOT BUSY WORK.)

ENERGY + MINDSET FOCUS:

(ONE VIBE, MANTRA, OR ENERGY YOU'RE CHOOSING TO LEAD WITH THIS WEEK.) _____

CELEBRATE YOUR DAMN WINS:

INNER WINS **(MINDSET + ENERGY)**	**ACTION WINS** **(SH*T YOU ACTUALLY DID)**	**ALIGNMENT WINS** **(SOUL-LEVEL YES MOMENTS)**
THE MOMENTS YOU CHOSE GROWTH, CALM, COURAGE, OR CLARITY OVER CHAOS.	TANGIBLE MOVES YOU MADE — BIG OR SMALL — THAT PROVE YOU'RE BUILDING MOMENTUM.	WHEN SOMETHING FELT RIGHT, EASY, ALIGNED, OR JOYFULLY YOU.

WHAT NEEDS TO **SHIFT** ASAP?

HOW WAS MY **SLEEP LAST NIGHT**

1 2 3 4 5 6 7 8 9 10

HOW **MOTIVATED** DO I FEEL TODAY

1 2 3 4 5 6 7 8 9 10

WHERE IS MY **PHYSICAL ENERGY LEVEL**

1 2 3 4 5 6 7 8 9 10

HOW IS MY **EMOTIONAL CAPACITY**

1 2 3 4 5 6 7 8 9 10

SHITTY ——————————————————— AWESOME

THREE THINGS I'M **GRATEFUL FOR:**

_____
_____
_____
_____
_____
_____
_____

REFLECTION OF YESTERDAY

DID I DO THE THINGS I **COMMITED** TO DO?   (Y) (N)

DID I DO SOMETHING FOR **MYSELF**? (joy, rest, movement, fun)   (Y) (N)

DID I PROTECT MY **ENERGY** AND SET **CLEAR BOUNDARIES**?   (Y) (N)

DID I **CELEBRATE** A SMALL WIN (or acknowledge progress)   (Y) (N)

DID I CHECK IN WITH MY **VISION + GOALS** (even briefly)?   (Y) (N)

DID I MAKE AT LEAST ONE **BOLD MOVE** OR **CEO DECISION**?   (Y) (N)

DID I **STAY FOCUSED** ON MY GROWTH?   (Y) (N)

IF I ANSWERED "NO" TO ANY **WHAT DO I SHIFT TODAY**?

_____
_____
_____
_____
_____

3 **ACTION STEPS** (COMMITMENTS) I WILL DO TODAY
THINGS YOU WILL COMMIT TO YOURSELF AND YOUR BUSINESS TO SUPPORT YOUR VISION

SOMETHING I NEED TO **REMIND MYSELF** OF TODAY _____

BUSINESS TO DO LIST:

PERSONAL TO DO LIST:

TOP PRIORITIES TODAY

_____

_____

_____

_____

HOW MUCH **TIME** WILL I
DEDICATE TO MY BUSINESS
TODAY?

6 am

7 am

8 am

9 am

10 am

11 am

12 pm

1 pm

2 pm

3 pm

4 pm

5 pm

6 pm

7 pm

HOW WAS MY **SLEEP LAST NIGHT**

1 2 3 4 5 6 7 8 9 10

HOW **MOTIVATED** DO I FEEL TODAY

1 2 3 4 5 6 7 8 9 10

WHERE IS MY **PHYSICAL ENERGY LEVEL**

1 2 3 4 5 6 7 8 9 10

HOW IS MY **EMOTIONAL CAPACITY**

1 2 3 4 5 6 7 8 9 10

SHITTY ———————————————— AWESOME

THREE THINGS I'M
GRATEFUL FOR:

REFLECTION OF YESTERDAY

DID I DO THE THINGS I **COMMITED** TO DO? Y N

DID I DO SOMETHING FOR **MYSELF**? (joy, rest, movement, fun) Y N

DID I PROTECT MY **ENERGY** AND SET **CLEAR BOUNDARIES**? Y N

DID I **CELEBRATE** A SMALL WIN (or acknowledge progress) Y N

DID I CHECK IN WITH MY **VISION + GOALS** (even briefly)? Y N

DID I MAKE AT LEAST ONE **BOLD MOVE** OR **CEO DECISION**? Y N

DID I **STAY FOCUSED** ON MY GROWTH? Y N

IF I ANSWERED "NO" TO ANY
WHAT DO I SHIFT TODAY?

---

3 ACTION STEPS (COMMITMENTS) I WILL DO TODAY
THINGS YOU WILL COMMIT TO YOURSELF AND YOUR BUSINESS TO SUPPORT YOUR VISION

SOMETHING I NEED TO **REMIND MYSELF** OF TODAY

BUSINESS TO DO LIST:

PERSONAL TO DO LIST:

TOP PRIORITIES TODAY

_____

_____

_____

HOW MUCH **TIME** WILL I DEDICATE TO MY BUSINESS TODAY?

6 am

7 am

8 am

9 am

10 am

11 am

12 pm

1 pm

2 pm

3 pm

4 pm

5 pm

6 pm

7 pm

HOW WAS MY **SLEEP LAST NIGHT**

① ② ③ ④ ⑤ ⑥ ⑦ ⑧ ⑨ ⑩

HOW **MOTIVATED** DO I FEEL TODAY

① ② ③ ④ ⑤ ⑥ ⑦ ⑧ ⑨ ⑩

WHERE IS MY **PHYSICAL ENERGY LEVEL**

① ② ③ ④ ⑤ ⑥ ⑦ ⑧ ⑨ ⑩

HOW IS MY **EMOTIONAL CAPACITY**

① ② ③ ④ ⑤ ⑥ ⑦ ⑧ ⑨ ⑩

SHITTY ——————————————— AWESOME

THREE THINGS I'M **GRATEFUL FOR:**

_____
_____
_____
_____
_____
_____
_____

REFLECTION OF YESTERDAY

DID I DO THE THINGS I **COMMITED** TO DO? Ⓨ Ⓝ

DID I DO SOMETHING FOR **MYSELF**? (joy, rest, movement, fun) Ⓨ Ⓝ

DID I PROTECT MY **ENERGY** AND SET **CLEAR BOUNDARIES**? Ⓨ Ⓝ

DID I **CELEBRATE** A SMALL WIN (or acknowledge progress) Ⓨ Ⓝ

DID I CHECK IN WITH MY **VISION + GOALS** (even briefly)? Ⓨ Ⓝ

DID I MAKE AT LEAST ONE **BOLD MOVE** OR **CEO DECISION**? Ⓨ Ⓝ

DID I **STAY FOCUSED** ON MY GROWTH? Ⓨ Ⓝ

IF I ANSWERED "NO" TO ANY **WHAT DO I SHIFT TODAY**?

_____
_____
_____
_____

3 ACTION STEPS (COMMITMENTS) I WILL DO TODAY

THINGS YOU WILL COMMIT TO YOURSELF AND YOUR BUSINESS TO SUPPORT YOUR VISION

SOMETHING I NEED TO **REMIND MYSELF** OF TODAY _____

BUSINESS TO DO LIST:

PERSONAL TO DO LIST:

TOP PRIORITIES TODAY

_____

_____

_____

_____

HOW MUCH **TIME** WILL I DEDICATE TO MY BUSINESS TODAY?

6 am

7 am

8 am

9 am

10 am

11 am

12 pm

1 pm

2 pm

3 pm

4 pm

5 pm

6 pm

7 pm

HOW WAS MY **SLEEP LAST NIGHT**

1 2 3 4 5 6 7 8 9 10

HOW **MOTIVATED** DO I FEEL TODAY

1 2 3 4 5 6 7 8 9 10

WHERE IS MY **PHYSICAL ENERGY LEVEL**

1 2 3 4 5 6 7 8 9 10

HOW IS MY **EMOTIONAL CAPACITY**

1 2 3 4 5 6 7 8 9 10

SHITTY ———————————————— AWESOME

THREE THINGS I'M
GRATEFUL FOR:

REFLECTION OF YESTERDAY

	Y	N
DID I DO THE THINGS I **COMMITED** TO DO?	Y	N
DID I DO SOMETHING FOR **MYSELF**? (joy, rest, movement, fun)	Y	N
DID I PROTECT MY **ENERGY** AND SET **CLEAR BOUNDARIES**?	Y	N
DID I **CELEBRATE** A SMALL WIN (or acknowledge progress)	Y	N
DID I CHECK IN WITH MY **VISION + GOALS** (even briefly)?	Y	N
DID I MAKE AT LEAST ONE **BOLD MOVE** OR **CEO DECISION**?	Y	N
DID I **STAY FOCUSED** ON MY GROWTH?	Y	N

IF I ANSWERED "NO" TO ANY
WHAT DO I SHIFT TODAY?

---

3 ACTION STEPS (COMMITMENTS) I WILL DO TODAY
THINGS YOU WILL COMMIT TO YOURSELF AND YOUR BUSINESS TO SUPPORT YOUR VISION

SOMETHING I NEED TO **REMIND MYSELF** OF TODAY _____

BUSINESS TO DO LIST:

PERSONAL TO DO LIST:

TOP PRIORITIES TODAY

_____

_____

_____

HOW MUCH **TIME** WILL I DEDICATE TO MY BUSINESS TODAY?

6 am

7 am

8 am

9 am

10 am

11 am

12 pm

1 pm

2 pm

3 pm

4 pm

5 pm

6 pm

7 pm

She's the
STRATEGY
Unapologetically Authentic. Own That Damn Business

JAN   FEB   MAR   APR   MAY   JUN   JUL   AUG   SEP   OCT   NOV   DEC   20___
1 2 3 4 5 6 7 8 9 10 11 12 13 14 15 16 17 18 19 20 21 22 23 24 25 26 27 28 29 30 31

HOW WAS MY **SLEEP LAST NIGHT**

① ② ③ ④ ⑤ ⑥ ⑦ ⑧ ⑨ ⑩

HOW **MOTIVATED** DO I FEEL TODAY

① ② ③ ④ ⑤ ⑥ ⑦ ⑧ ⑨ ⑩

WHERE IS MY **PHYSICAL ENERGY LEVEL**

① ② ③ ④ ⑤ ⑥ ⑦ ⑧ ⑨ ⑩

HOW IS MY **EMOTIONAL CAPACITY**

① ② ③ ④ ⑤ ⑥ ⑦ ⑧ ⑨ ⑩

SHITTY ——————————————————— AWESOME

THREE THINGS I'M **GRATEFUL FOR:**

_____
_____
_____
_____
_____
_____
_____

REFLECTION OF YESTERDAY

DID I DO THE THINGS I **COMMITED** TO DO? (Y)(N)

DID I DO SOMETHING FOR **MYSELF**? (joy, rest, movement, fun) (Y)(N)

DID I PROTECT MY **ENERGY** AND SET **CLEAR BOUNDARIES**? (Y)(N)

DID I **CELEBRATE** A SMALL WIN (or acknowledge progress) (Y)(N)

DID I CHECK IN WITH MY **VISION + GOALS** (even briefly)? (Y)(N)

DID I MAKE AT LEAST ONE **BOLD MOVE** OR **CEO DECISION**? (Y)(N)

DID I **STAY FOCUSED** ON MY GROWTH? (Y)(N)

IF I ANSWERED "NO" TO ANY
WHAT DO I SHIFT TODAY?

_____
_____
_____
_____
_____

3 **ACTION STEPS** (COMMITMENTS) I WILL DO TODAY
THINGS YOU WILL COMMIT TO YOURSELF AND YOUR BUSINESS TO SUPPORT YOUR VISION

SOMETHING I NEED TO **REMIND MYSELF** OF TODAY _____

BUSINESS TO DO LIST:

PERSONAL TO DO LIST:

TOP PRIORITIES TODAY

_____

_____

_____

HOW MUCH **TIME** WILL I DEDICATE TO MY BUSINESS TODAY?

6 am

7 am

8 am

9 am

10 am

11 am

12 pm

1 pm

2 pm

3 pm

4 pm

5 pm

6 pm

7 pm

HOW WAS MY **SLEEP LAST NIGHT**

(1) (2) (3) (4) (5) (6) (7) (8) (9) (10)

HOW **MOTIVATED** DO I FEEL TODAY

(1) (2) (3) (4) (5) (6) (7) (8) (9) (10)

WHERE IS MY **PHYSICAL ENERGY LEVEL**

(1) (2) (3) (4) (5) (6) (7) (8) (9) (10)

HOW IS MY **EMOTIONAL CAPACITY**

(1) (2) (3) (4) (5) (6) (7) (8) (9) (10)

SHITTY ———————————————— AWESOME

THREE THINGS I'M **GRATEFUL FOR:**

_____
_____
_____
_____
_____
_____
_____
_____

REFLECTION OF YESTERDAY

DID I DO THE THINGS I **COMMITED** TO DO? (Y) (N)

DID I DO SOMETHING FOR **MYSELF**? (joy, rest, movement, fun) (Y) (N)

DID I PROTECT MY **ENERGY** AND SET **CLEAR BOUNDARIES**? (Y) (N)

DID I **CELEBRATE** A SMALL WIN (or acknowledge progress) (Y) (N)

DID I CHECK IN WITH MY **VISION + GOALS** (even briefly)? (Y) (N)

DID I MAKE AT LEAST ONE **BOLD MOVE** OR **CEO DECISION**? (Y) (N)

DID I **STAY FOCUSED** ON MY GROWTH? (Y) (N)

IF I ANSWERED "NO" TO ANY **WHAT DO I SHIFT TODAY**?

_____
_____
_____
_____
_____

3 **ACTION STEPS** (COMMITMENTS) I WILL DO TODAY

THINGS YOU WILL COMMIT TO YOURSELF AND YOUR BUSINESS TO SUPPORT YOUR VISION

SOMETHING I NEED TO **REMIND MYSELF** OF TODAY _____

BUSINESS TO DO LIST:

PERSONAL TO DO LIST:

TOP PRIORITIES TODAY

_____

_____

_____

_____

HOW MUCH **TIME** WILL I DEDICATE TO MY BUSINESS TODAY?

6 am

7 am

8 am

9 am

10 am

11 am

12 pm

1 pm

2 pm

3 pm

4 pm

5 pm

6 pm

7 pm

HOW WAS MY **SLEEP LAST NIGHT**

1 2 3 4 5 6 7 8 9 10

HOW **MOTIVATED** DO I FEEL TODAY

1 2 3 4 5 6 7 8 9 10

WHERE IS MY **PHYSICAL ENERGY LEVEL**

1 2 3 4 5 6 7 8 9 10

HOW IS MY **EMOTIONAL CAPACITY**

1 2 3 4 5 6 7 8 9 10

SHITTY ———————————— AWESOME

THREE THINGS I'M
GRATEFUL FOR:

REFLECTION OF YESTERDAY

DID I DO THE THINGS I **COMMITED** TO DO?   Y N

DID I DO SOMETHING FOR **MYSELF**? (joy, rest, movement, fun)   Y N

DID I PROTECT MY **ENERGY** AND SET **CLEAR BOUNDARIES**?   Y N

DID I **CELEBRATE** A SMALL WIN (or acknowledge progress)   Y N

DID I CHECK IN WITH MY **VISION + GOALS** (even briefly)?   Y N

DID I MAKE AT LEAST ONE **BOLD MOVE** OR **CEO DECISION**?   Y N

DID I **STAY FOCUSED** ON MY GROWTH?   Y N

IF I ANSWERED "NO" TO ANY
WHAT DO I SHIFT TODAY?

3 ACTION STEPS (COMMITMENTS) I WILL DO TODAY
THINGS YOU WILL COMMIT TO YOURSELF AND YOUR BUSINESS TO SUPPORT YOUR VISION

SOMETHING I NEED TO **REMIND MYSELF** OF TODAY

BUSINESS TO DO LIST:

PERSONAL TO DO LIST:

TOP PRIORITIES TODAY

_____

_____

_____

_____

HOW MUCH **TIME** WILL I
DEDICATE TO MY BUSINESS
TODAY?

6 am

7 am

8 am

9 am

10 am

11 am

12 pm

1 pm

2 pm

3 pm

4 pm

5 pm

6 pm

7 pm

WEEKLY CHECK-IN

PERSONAL ENERGY & WELL-BEING
On a scale of 1–10, how would I rate...

MY OVERALL **ENERGY** THIS WEEK

(1) (2) (3) (4) (5) (6) (7) (8) (9) (10)

MY **EMOTIONAL CAPACITY** THIS WEEK

(1) (2) (3) (4) (5) (6) (7) (8) (9) (10)

MY **MOTIVATION + CLARITY** THIS WEEK

(1) (2) (3) (4) (5) (6) (7) (8) (9) (10)

SHITTY ———————————————————— AWESOME

WHAT SUPPORTED MY WELL-BEING THIS WEEK?

WHAT DRAINED ME THAT I WANT TO SHIFT OR ELIMINATE?

WHAT DID I DO JUST FOR ME THIS WEEK?

BUSINESS & LEADERSHIP REFLECTIONS

DID I **STAY FOCUSED** ON MY TOP PRIORITIES? (Y) (N)

DID I **LEAD** WITH CONFIDENCE, EVEN WHEN IT WAS HARD? (Y) (N)

DID I **SHOW UP** FOR MY BRAND IN A WAY I'M PROUD OF? (Y) (N)

DID I COMMUNICATE **CLEAR BOUNDARIES** AROUND MY TIME? (Y) (N)

WHAT WORKED REALLY WELL IN MY BUSINESS THIS WEEK?

WHAT CHALLENGES CAME UP, AND WHAT DID I LEARN FROM THEM?

WHAT BOLD MOVE DID I MAKE (OR WISH I HAD)?

ALIGNMENT & INTENTION

AM I STILL MOVING TOWARD MY BIGGER VISION — OR AM I JUST STAYING BUSY?

WHAT DO I NEED TO PAUSE, PIVOT, OR RELEASE RIGHT NOW?

WHAT'S ONE THING I WANT TO RECOMMIT TO NEXT WEEK?

NEXT WEEK'S FOCUS

ONE BOLD THING I'LL DO THIS WEEK

ONE BOUNDARY I'LL PROTECT

WEEKLY **GOAL PLANNER** LIKE A
DAMN BUSINESS BADASS

MY **WEEKLY** FOCUS

TOP 3 POWER GOALS FOR THIS WEEK - (WHAT ACTUALLY MOVES THE NEEDLE — NOT BUSY WORK.)

ENERGY + MINDSET FOCUS:

(ONE VIBE, MANTRA, OR ENERGY YOU'RE CHOOSING TO LEAD WITH THIS WEEK.) _____

CELEBRATE YOUR DAMN WINS:

INNER WINS **(MINDSET + ENERGY)** THE MOMENTS YOU CHOSE GROWTH, CALM, COURAGE, OR CLARITY OVER CHAOS.	**ACTION WINS** **(SH*T YOU ACTUALLY DID)** TANGIBLE MOVES YOU MADE — BIG OR SMALL — THAT PROVE YOU'RE BUILDING MOMENTUM.	**ALIGNMENT WINS** **(SOUL-LEVEL YES MOMENTS)** WHEN SOMETHING FELT RIGHT, EASY, ALIGNED, OR JOYFULLY YOU.

WHAT NEEDS TO **SHIFT** ASAP?

HOW WAS MY **SLEEP LAST NIGHT**

1 2 3 4 5 6 7 8 9 10

HOW **MOTIVATED** DO I FEEL TODAY

1 2 3 4 5 6 7 8 9 10

WHERE IS MY **PHYSICAL ENERGY LEVEL**

1 2 3 4 5 6 7 8 9 10

HOW IS MY **EMOTIONAL CAPACITY**

1 2 3 4 5 6 7 8 9 10

SHITTY ——————————————— AWESOME

THREE THINGS I'M
GRATEFUL FOR:

REFLECTION OF YESTERDAY

DID I DO THE THINGS I **COMMITED** TO DO? Y N

DID I DO SOMETHING FOR **MYSELF**? (joy, rest, movement, fun) Y N

DID I PROTECT MY **ENERGY** AND SET **CLEAR BOUNDARIES**? Y N

DID I **CELEBRATE** A SMALL WIN (or acknowledge progress) Y N

DID I CHECK IN WITH MY **VISION + GOALS** (even briefly)? Y N

DID I MAKE AT LEAST ONE **BOLD MOVE** OR **CEO DECISION**? Y N

DID I **STAY FOCUSED** ON MY GROWTH? Y N

IF I ANSWERED "NO" TO ANY
WHAT DO I SHIFT TODAY?

3 ACTION STEPS (COMMITMENTS) I WILL DO TODAY

THINGS YOU WILL COMMIT TO YOURSELF AND YOUR BUSINESS TO SUPPORT YOUR VISION

SOMETHING I NEED TO **REMIND MYSELF** OF TODAY

BUSINESS TO DO LIST:

PERSONAL TO DO LIST:

TOP PRIORITIES TODAY

_____
_____
_____

HOW MUCH **TIME** WILL I DEDICATE TO MY BUSINESS TODAY?

6 am

7 am

8 am

9 am

10 am

11 am

12 pm

1 pm

2 pm

3 pm

4 pm

5 pm

6 pm

7 pm

HOW WAS MY **SLEEP LAST NIGHT**

(1) (2) (3) (4) (5) (6) (7) (8) (9) (10)

HOW **MOTIVATED** DO I FEEL TODAY

(1) (2) (3) (4) (5) (6) (7) (8) (9) (10)

WHERE IS MY **PHYSICAL ENERGY LEVEL**

(1) (2) (3) (4) (5) (6) (7) (8) (9) (10)

HOW IS MY **EMOTIONAL CAPACITY**

(1) (2) (3) (4) (5) (6) (7) (8) (9) (10)

SHITTY ——————————————— AWESOME

THREE THINGS I'M **GRATEFUL FOR:**

_____
_____
_____
_____
_____
_____
_____

REFLECTION OF YESTERDAY

DID I DO THE THINGS I **COMMITED** TO DO? (Y) (N)

DID I DO SOMETHING FOR **MYSELF**? (joy, rest, movement, fun) (Y) (N)

DID I PROTECT MY **ENERGY** AND SET **CLEAR BOUNDARIES**? (Y) (N)

DID I **CELEBRATE** A SMALL WIN (or acknowledge progress) (Y) (N)

DID I CHECK IN WITH MY **VISION + GOALS** (even briefly)? (Y) (N)

DID I MAKE AT LEAST ONE **BOLD MOVE** OR **CEO DECISION**? (Y) (N)

DID I **STAY FOCUSED** ON MY GROWTH? (Y) (N)

IF I ANSWERED "NO" TO ANY **WHAT DO I SHIFT TODAY**?

_____
_____
_____
_____
_____

3 ACTION STEPS (COMMITMENTS) I WILL DO TODAY
THINGS YOU WILL COMMIT TO YOURSELF AND YOUR BUSINESS TO SUPPORT YOUR VISION

SOMETHING I NEED TO **REMIND MYSELF** OF TODAY _____

_____

BUSINESS TO DO LIST:

PERSONAL TO DO LIST:

TOP PRIORITIES TODAY

_____

_____

_____

HOW MUCH **TIME** WILL I
DEDICATE TO MY BUSINESS
TODAY?

6 am

7 am

8 am

9 am

10 am

11 am

12 pm

1 pm

2 pm

3 pm

4 pm

5 pm

6 pm

7 pm

She's the STRATEGY

HOW WAS MY SLEEP LAST NIGHT

(1) (2) (3) (4) (5) (6) (7) (8) (9) (10)

HOW MOTIVATED DO I FEEL TODAY

(1) (2) (3) (4) (5) (6) (7) (8) (9) (10)

WHERE IS MY PHYSICAL ENERGY LEVEL

(1) (2) (3) (4) (5) (6) (7) (8) (9) (10)

HOW IS MY EMOTIONAL CAPACITY

(1) (2) (3) (4) (5) (6) (7) (8) (9) (10)

SHITTY ————————————————— AWESOME

THREE THINGS I'M **GRATEFUL FOR:**

REFLECTION OF YESTERDAY

	Y N
DID I DO THE THINGS I **COMMITED** TO DO?	Y N
DID I DO SOMETHING FOR **MYSELF**? (joy, rest, movement, fun)	Y N
DID I PROTECT MY **ENERGY** AND SET **CLEAR BOUNDARIES**?	Y N
DID I **CELEBRATE** A SMALL WIN (or acknowledge progress)	Y N
DID I CHECK IN WITH MY **VISION + GOALS** (even briefly)?	Y N
DID I MAKE AT LEAST ONE **BOLD MOVE** OR **CEO DECISION**?	Y N
DID I **STAY FOCUSED** ON MY GROWTH?	Y N

IF I ANSWERED "NO" TO ANY
WHAT DO I SHIFT TODAY?

3 ACTION STEPS (COMMITMENTS) I WILL DO TODAY

THINGS YOU WILL COMMIT TO YOURSELF AND YOUR BUSINESS TO SUPPORT YOUR VISION

SOMETHING I NEED TO **REMIND MYSELF** OF TODAY

BUSINESS TO DO LIST:

PERSONAL TO DO LIST:

TOP PRIORITIES TODAY

_____

_____

_____

HOW MUCH **TIME** WILL I
DEDICATE TO MY BUSINESS
TODAY?

6 am

7 am

8 am

9 am

10 am

11 am

12 pm

1 pm

2 pm

3 pm

4 pm

5 pm

6 pm

7 pm

HOW WAS MY SLEEP LAST NIGHT

(1) (2) (3) (4) (5) (6) (7) (8) (9) (10)

HOW MOTIVATED DO I FEEL TODAY

(1) (2) (3) (4) (5) (6) (7) (8) (9) (10)

WHERE IS MY PHYSICAL ENERGY LEVEL

(1) (2) (3) (4) (5) (6) (7) (8) (9) (10)

HOW IS MY EMOTIONAL CAPACITY

(1) (2) (3) (4) (5) (6) (7) (8) (9) (10)

SHITTY ——————————————————— AWESOME

THREE THINGS I'M GRATEFUL FOR:

_____

_____

_____

_____

_____

_____

REFLECTION OF YESTERDAY

DID I DO THE THINGS I **COMMITED** TO DO? (Y)(N)

DID I DO SOMETHING FOR **MYSELF**? (joy, rest, movement, fun) (Y)(N)

DID I PROTECT MY **ENERGY** AND SET **CLEAR BOUNDARIES**? (Y)(N)

DID I **CELEBRATE** A SMALL WIN (or acknowledge progress) (Y)(N)

DID I CHECK IN WITH MY **VISION + GOALS** (even briefly)? (Y)(N)

DID I MAKE AT LEAST ONE **BOLD MOVE** OR **CEO DECISION**? (Y)(N)

DID I **STAY FOCUSED** ON MY GROWTH? (Y)(N)

IF I ANSWERED "NO" TO ANY
WHAT DO I SHIFT TODAY?

_____

_____

_____

_____

3 ACTION STEPS (COMMITMENTS) I WILL DO TODAY
THINGS YOU WILL COMMIT TO YOURSELF AND YOUR BUSINESS TO SUPPORT YOUR VISION

SOMETHING I NEED TO **REMIND MYSELF** OF TODAY _____

BUSINESS TO DO LIST:

PERSONAL TO DO LIST:

TOP PRIORITIES TODAY

_____

_____

_____

HOW MUCH **TIME** WILL I DEDICATE TO MY BUSINESS TODAY?

6 am

7 am

8 am

9 am

10 am

11 am

12 pm

1 pm

2 pm

3 pm

4 pm

5 pm

6 pm

7 pm

HOW WAS MY **SLEEP LAST NIGHT**

(1) (2) (3) (4) (5) (6) (7) (8) (9) (10)

HOW **MOTIVATED** DO I FEEL TODAY

(1) (2) (3) (4) (5) (6) (7) (8) (9) (10)

WHERE IS MY **PHYSICAL ENERGY LEVEL**

(1) (2) (3) (4) (5) (6) (7) (8) (9) (10)

HOW IS MY **EMOTIONAL CAPACITY**

(1) (2) (3) (4) (5) (6) (7) (8) (9) (10)

SHITTY ——————————————— AWESOME

THREE THINGS I'M **GRATEFUL FOR:**

_____

_____

_____

_____

_____

_____

_____

REFLECTION OF YESTERDAY

DID I DO THE THINGS I **COMMITED** TO DO? (Y) (N)

DID I DO SOMETHING FOR **MYSELF**? (joy, rest, movement, fun) (Y) (N)

DID I PROTECT MY **ENERGY** AND SET **CLEAR BOUNDARIES**? (Y) (N)

DID I **CELEBRATE** A SMALL WIN (or acknowledge progress) (Y) (N)

DID I CHECK IN WITH MY **VISION + GOALS** (even briefly)? (Y) (N)

DID I MAKE AT LEAST ONE **BOLD MOVE** OR **CEO DECISION**? (Y) (N)

DID I **STAY FOCUSED** ON MY GROWTH? (Y) (N)

IF I ANSWERED "NO" TO ANY **WHAT DO I SHIFT TODAY**?

_____

_____

_____

_____

3 ACTION STEPS (COMMITMENTS) I WILL DO TODAY
THINGS YOU WILL COMMIT TO YOURSELF AND YOUR BUSINESS TO SUPPORT YOUR VISION

SOMETHING I NEED TO **REMIND MYSELF** OF TODAY _____

BUSINESS TO DO LIST:

PERSONAL TO DO LIST:

TOP PRIORITIES TODAY

_____

_____

_____

_____

HOW MUCH **TIME** WILL I DEDICATE TO MY BUSINESS TODAY?

6 am

7 am

8 am

9 am

10 am

11 am

12 pm

1 pm

2 pm

3 pm

4 pm

5 pm

6 pm

7 pm

HOW WAS MY **SLEEP LAST NIGHT**

(1) (2) (3) (4) (5) (6) (7) (8) (9) (10)

HOW **MOTIVATED** DO I FEEL TODAY

(1) (2) (3) (4) (5) (6) (7) (8) (9) (10)

WHERE IS MY **PHYSICAL ENERGY LEVEL**

(1) (2) (3) (4) (5) (6) (7) (8) (9) (10)

HOW IS MY **EMOTIONAL CAPACITY**

(1) (2) (3) (4) (5) (6) (7) (8) (9) (10)

SHITTY ——————————————— AWESOME

THREE THINGS I'M **GRATEFUL FOR:**

_____
_____
_____
_____
_____
_____
_____

REFLECTION OF YESTERDAY

DID I DO THE THINGS I **COMMITED** TO DO? (Y)(N)

DID I DO SOMETHING FOR **MYSELF**? (joy, rest, movement, fun) (Y)(N)

DID I PROTECT MY **ENERGY** AND SET **CLEAR BOUNDARIES**? (Y)(N)

DID I **CELEBRATE** A SMALL WIN (or acknowledge progress) (Y)(N)

DID I CHECK IN WITH MY **VISION + GOALS** (even briefly)? (Y)(N)

DID I MAKE AT LEAST ONE **BOLD MOVE** OR **CEO DECISION**? (Y)(N)

DID I **STAY FOCUSED** ON MY GROWTH? (Y)(N)

IF I ANSWERED "NO" TO ANY **WHAT DO I SHIFT TODAY**?

_____
_____
_____
_____
_____

---

3 ACTION STEPS (COMMITMENTS) I WILL DO TODAY

THINGS YOU WILL COMMIT TO YOURSELF AND YOUR BUSINESS TO SUPPORT YOUR VISION

SOMETHING I NEED TO **REMIND MYSELF** OF TODAY _____

BUSINESS TO DO LIST:

PERSONAL TO DO LIST:

TOP PRIORITIES TODAY

_____

_____

_____

HOW MUCH **TIME** WILL I
DEDICATE TO MY BUSINESS
TODAY?

6 am

7 am

8 am

9 am

10 am

11 am

12 pm

1 pm

2 pm

3 pm

4 pm

5 pm

6 pm

7 pm

HOW WAS MY **SLEEP LAST NIGHT**

(1) (2) (3) (4) (5) (6) (7) (8) (9) (10)

HOW **MOTIVATED** DO I FEEL TODAY

(1) (2) (3) (4) (5) (6) (7) (8) (9) (10)

WHERE IS MY **PHYSICAL ENERGY LEVEL**

(1) (2) (3) (4) (5) (6) (7) (8) (9) (10)

HOW IS MY **EMOTIONAL CAPACITY**

(1) (2) (3) (4) (5) (6) (7) (8) (9) (10)

SHITTY ———————————————— AWESOME

THREE THINGS I'M **GRATEFUL FOR:**

_____
_____
_____
_____
_____
_____
_____

REFLECTION OF YESTERDAY

DID I DO THE THINGS I **COMMITED** TO DO? (Y) (N)

DID I DO SOMETHING FOR **MYSELF**? (joy, rest, movement, fun) (Y) (N)

DID I PROTECT MY **ENERGY** AND SET **CLEAR BOUNDARIES**? (Y) (N)

DID I **CELEBRATE** A SMALL WIN (or acknowledge progress) (Y) (N)

DID I CHECK IN WITH MY **VISION + GOALS** (even briefly)? (Y) (N)

DID I MAKE AT LEAST ONE **BOLD MOVE** OR **CEO DECISION**? (Y) (N)

DID I **STAY FOCUSED** ON MY GROWTH? (Y) (N)

IF I ANSWERED "NO" TO ANY **WHAT DO I SHIFT TODAY**?

_____
_____
_____
_____
_____

3 **ACTION STEPS** (COMMITMENTS) I WILL DO TODAY

THINGS YOU WILL COMMIT TO YOURSELF AND YOUR BUSINESS TO SUPPORT YOUR VISION

SOMETHING I NEED TO **REMIND MYSELF** OF TODAY _____

BUSINESS TO DO LIST:

PERSONAL TO DO LIST:

TOP PRIORITIES TODAY

_____

_____

_____

_____

HOW MUCH **TIME** WILL I DEDICATE TO MY BUSINESS TODAY?

6 am

7 am

8 am

9 am

10 am

11 am

12 pm

1 pm

2 pm

3 pm

4 pm

5 pm

6 pm

7 pm

WEEKLY CHECK-IN

PERSONAL ENERGY & WELL-BEING
On a scale of 1–10, how would I rate...

MY OVERALL **ENERGY** THIS WEEK

(1) (2) (3) (4) (5) (6) (7) (8) (9) (10)

MY **EMOTIONAL CAPACITY** THIS WEEK

(1) (2) (3) (4) (5) (6) (7) (8) (9) (10)

MY **MOTIVATION + CLARITY** THIS WEEK

(1) (2) (3) (4) (5) (6) (7) (8) (9) (10)

SHITTY ———————————————— AWESOME

WHAT SUPPORTED MY WELL-BEING THIS WEEK?

_____

_____

WHAT DRAINED ME THAT I WANT TO SHIFT OR ELIMINATE?

_____

_____

WHAT DID I DO JUST FOR ME THIS WEEK?

_____

_____

BUSINESS & LEADERSHIP REFLECTIONS

DID I **STAY FOCUSED** ON MY TOP PRIORITIES? (Y) (N)

DID I **LEAD** WITH CONFIDENCE, EVEN WHEN IT WAS HARD? (Y) (N)

DID I **SHOW UP** FOR MY BRAND IN A WAY I'M PROUD OF? (Y) (N)

DID I COMMUNICATE **CLEAR BOUNDARIES** AROUND MY TIME? (Y) (N)

WHAT WORKED REALLY WELL IN MY BUSINESS THIS WEEK?

_____

WHAT CHALLENGES CAME UP, AND WHAT DID I LEARN FROM THEM?

_____

WHAT BOLD MOVE DID I MAKE (OR WISH I HAD)?

_____

ALIGNMENT & INTENTION

AM I STILL MOVING TOWARD MY BIGGER VISION — OR AM I JUST STAYING BUSY?

WHAT DO I NEED TO PAUSE, PIVOT, OR RELEASE RIGHT NOW?

WHAT'S ONE THING I WANT TO RECOMMIT TO NEXT WEEK?

NEXT WEEK'S FOCUS

ONE BOLD THING I'LL DO THIS WEEK

ONE BOUNDARY I'LL PROTECT

WEEKLY **GOAL PLANNER** LIKE A
DAMN BUSINESS BADASS

MY **WEEKLY** FOCUS
TOP 3 POWER GOALS FOR THIS WEEK - (WHAT ACTUALLY MOVES THE NEEDLE — NOT BUSY WORK.)

ENERGY + MINDSET FOCUS:

(ONE VIBE, MANTRA, OR ENERGY YOU'RE CHOOSING TO LEAD WITH THIS WEEK.) _____

CELEBRATE YOUR DAMN WINS:

INNER WINS **(MINDSET + ENERGY)** THE MOMENTS YOU CHOSE GROWTH, CALM, COURAGE, OR CLARITY OVER CHAOS.	**ACTION WINS** **(SH*T YOU ACTUALLY DID)** TANGIBLE MOVES YOU MADE — BIG OR SMALL — THAT PROVE YOU'RE BUILDING MOMENTUM.	**ALIGNMENT WINS** **(SOUL-LEVEL YES MOMENTS)** WHEN SOMETHING FELT RIGHT, EASY, ALIGNED, OR JOYFULLY YOU.

WHAT NEEDS TO **SHIFT** ASAP?

HOW WAS MY **SLEEP LAST NIGHT**

① ② ③ ④ ⑤ ⑥ ⑦ ⑧ ⑨ ⑩

HOW **MOTIVATED** DO I FEEL TODAY

① ② ③ ④ ⑤ ⑥ ⑦ ⑧ ⑨ ⑩

WHERE IS MY **PHYSICAL ENERGY LEVEL**

① ② ③ ④ ⑤ ⑥ ⑦ ⑧ ⑨ ⑩

HOW IS MY **EMOTIONAL CAPACITY**

① ② ③ ④ ⑤ ⑥ ⑦ ⑧ ⑨ ⑩

SHITTY ————————————————— AWESOME

THREE THINGS I'M **GRATEFUL FOR:**

_____
_____
_____
_____
_____
_____
_____
_____

REFLECTION OF YESTERDAY

DID I DO THE THINGS I **COMMITED** TO DO? Ⓨ Ⓝ

DID I DO SOMETHING FOR **MYSELF**? (joy, rest, movement, fun) Ⓨ Ⓝ

DID I PROTECT MY **ENERGY** AND SET **CLEAR BOUNDARIES**? Ⓨ Ⓝ

DID I **CELEBRATE** A SMALL WIN (or acknowledge progress) Ⓨ Ⓝ

DID I CHECK IN WITH MY **VISION + GOALS** (even briefly)? Ⓨ Ⓝ

DID I MAKE AT LEAST ONE **BOLD MOVE** OR **CEO DECISION**? Ⓨ Ⓝ

DID I **STAY FOCUSED** ON MY GROWTH? Ⓨ Ⓝ

IF I ANSWERED "NO" TO ANY **WHAT DO I SHIFT TODAY**?

_____
_____
_____
_____
_____

3 **ACTION STEPS** (COMMITMENTS) I WILL DO TODAY
THINGS YOU WILL COMMIT TO YOURSELF AND YOUR BUSINESS TO SUPPORT YOUR VISION

SOMETHING I NEED TO **REMIND MYSELF** OF TODAY _____

BUSINESS TO DO LIST:

PERSONAL TO DO LIST:

TOP PRIORITIES TODAY

_____

_____

_____

HOW MUCH **TIME** WILL I DEDICATE TO MY BUSINESS TODAY?

6 am

7 am

8 am

9 am

10 am

11 am

12 pm

1 pm

2 pm

3 pm

4 pm

5 pm

6 pm

7 pm

JAN   FEB   MAR   APR   MAY   JUN   JUL   AUG   SEP   OCT   NOV   DEC   20___
1 2 3 4 5 6 7 8 9 10 11 12 13 14 15 16 17 18 19 20 21 22 23 24 25 26 27 28 29 30 31

HOW WAS MY **SLEEP LAST NIGHT**

① ② ③ ④ ⑤ ⑥ ⑦ ⑧ ⑨ ⑩

HOW **MOTIVATED** DO I FEEL TODAY

① ② ③ ④ ⑤ ⑥ ⑦ ⑧ ⑨ ⑩

WHERE IS MY **PHYSICAL ENERGY LEVEL**

① ② ③ ④ ⑤ ⑥ ⑦ ⑧ ⑨ ⑩

HOW IS MY **EMOTIONAL CAPACITY**

① ② ③ ④ ⑤ ⑥ ⑦ ⑧ ⑨ ⑩

SHITTY ———————————————— AWESOME

THREE THINGS I'M
GRATEFUL FOR:

_____
_____
_____
_____
_____
_____

REFLECTION OF YESTERDAY

DID I DO THE THINGS I **COMMITED** TO DO?   Ⓨ Ⓝ

DID I DO SOMETHING FOR **MYSELF**? (joy, rest, movement, fun)   Ⓨ Ⓝ

DID I PROTECT MY **ENERGY** AND SET **CLEAR BOUNDARIES**?   Ⓨ Ⓝ

DID I **CELEBRATE** A SMALL WIN (or acknowledge progress)   Ⓨ Ⓝ

DID I CHECK IN WITH MY **VISION + GOALS** (even briefly)?   Ⓨ Ⓝ

DID I MAKE AT LEAST ONE **BOLD MOVE** OR **CEO DECISION**?   Ⓨ Ⓝ

DID I **STAY FOCUSED** ON MY GROWTH?   Ⓨ Ⓝ

IF I ANSWERED "NO" TO ANY
WHAT DO I SHIFT TODAY?

_____
_____
_____
_____
_____

3 ACTION STEPS (COMMITMENTS) I WILL DO TODAY
THINGS YOU WILL COMMIT TO YOURSELF AND YOUR BUSINESS TO SUPPORT YOUR VISION

SOMETHING I NEED TO **REMIND MYSELF** OF TODAY _____

BUSINESS TO DO LIST:

PERSONAL TO DO LIST:

TOP PRIORITIES TODAY

_____

_____

_____

HOW MUCH **TIME** WILL I
DEDICATE TO MY BUSINESS
TODAY?

6 am _____ ✓

7 am _____ ✓

8 am _____ ✓

9 am _____ ✓

10 am _____ ✓

11 am _____ ✓

12 pm _____ ✓

1 pm _____ ✓

2 pm _____ ✓

3 pm _____ ✓

4 pm _____ ✓

5 pm _____ ✓

6 pm _____ ✓

7 pm _____ ✓

HOW WAS MY **SLEEP LAST NIGHT**

① ② ③ ④ ⑤ ⑥ ⑦ ⑧ ⑨ ⑩

HOW **MOTIVATED** DO I FEEL TODAY

① ② ③ ④ ⑤ ⑥ ⑦ ⑧ ⑨ ⑩

WHERE IS MY **PHYSICAL ENERGY LEVEL**

① ② ③ ④ ⑤ ⑥ ⑦ ⑧ ⑨ ⑩

HOW IS MY **EMOTIONAL CAPACITY**

① ② ③ ④ ⑤ ⑥ ⑦ ⑧ ⑨ ⑩

SHITTY ———————————————— AWESOME

THREE THINGS I'M **GRATEFUL FOR:**

REFLECTION OF YESTERDAY

DID I DO THE THINGS I **COMMITED** TO DO? Ⓨ Ⓝ

DID I DO SOMETHING FOR **MYSELF**? (joy, rest, movement, fun) Ⓨ Ⓝ

DID I PROTECT MY **ENERGY** AND SET **CLEAR BOUNDARIES**? Ⓨ Ⓝ

DID I **CELEBRATE** A SMALL WIN (or acknowledge progress) Ⓨ Ⓝ

DID I CHECK IN WITH MY **VISION + GOALS** (even briefly)? Ⓨ Ⓝ

DID I MAKE AT LEAST ONE **BOLD MOVE** OR **CEO DECISION**? Ⓨ Ⓝ

DID I **STAY FOCUSED** ON MY GROWTH? Ⓨ Ⓝ

IF I ANSWERED "NO" TO ANY **WHAT DO I SHIFT TODAY**?

3 **ACTION STEPS** (COMMITMENTS) I WILL DO TODAY
THINGS YOU WILL COMMIT TO YOURSELF AND YOUR BUSINESS TO SUPPORT YOUR VISION

SOMETHING I NEED TO **REMIND MYSELF** OF TODAY

BUSINESS TO DO LIST:

PERSONAL TO DO LIST:

TOP PRIORITIES TODAY

_____

_____

_____

HOW MUCH **TIME** WILL I
DEDICATE TO MY BUSINESS
TODAY?

6 am

7 am

8 am

9 am

10 am

11 am

12 pm

1 pm

2 pm

3 pm

4 pm

5 pm

6 pm

7 pm

JAN   FEB   MAR   APR   MAY   JUN   JUL   AUG   SEP   OCT   NOV   DEC   20___
1 2 3 4 5 6 7 8 9 10 11 12 13 14 15 16 17 18 19 20 21 22 23 24 25 26 27 28 29 30 31

HOW WAS MY **SLEEP LAST NIGHT**

(1) (2) (3) (4) (5) (6) (7) (8) (9) (10)

HOW **MOTIVATED** DO I FEEL TODAY

(1) (2) (3) (4) (5) (6) (7) (8) (9) (10)

WHERE IS MY **PHYSICAL ENERGY LEVEL**

(1) (2) (3) (4) (5) (6) (7) (8) (9) (10)

HOW IS MY **EMOTIONAL CAPACITY**

(1) (2) (3) (4) (5) (6) (7) (8) (9) (10)

SHITTY ——————————————————— AWESOME

THREE THINGS I'M **GRATEFUL FOR:**

_____
_____
_____
_____
_____
_____
_____

REFLECTION OF YESTERDAY

DID I DO THE THINGS I **COMMITED** TO DO?   (Y) (N)

DID I DO SOMETHING FOR **MYSELF**? (joy, rest, movement, fun)   (Y) (N)

DID I PROTECT MY **ENERGY** AND SET **CLEAR BOUNDARIES**?   (Y) (N)

DID I **CELEBRATE** A SMALL WIN (or acknowledge progress)   (Y) (N)

DID I CHECK IN WITH MY **VISION + GOALS** (even briefly)?   (Y) (N)

DID I MAKE AT LEAST ONE **BOLD MOVE** OR **CEO DECISION**?   (Y) (N)

DID I **STAY FOCUSED** ON MY GROWTH?   (Y) (N)

IF I ANSWERED "NO" TO ANY **WHAT DO I SHIFT TODAY**?

_____
_____
_____
_____
_____

3 ACTION STEPS (COMMITMENTS) I WILL DO TODAY
THINGS YOU WILL COMMIT TO YOURSELF AND YOUR BUSINESS TO SUPPORT YOUR VISION

SOMETHING I NEED TO **REMIND MYSELF** OF TODAY _____

BUSINESS TO DO LIST:

PERSONAL TO DO LIST:

TOP PRIORITIES TODAY

_____
_____
_____
_____

HOW MUCH **TIME** WILL I DEDICATE TO MY BUSINESS TODAY?

6 am

7 am

8 am

9 am

10 am

11 am

12 pm

1 pm

2 pm

3 pm

4 pm

5 pm

6 pm

7 pm

She's the STRATEGY
Unapologetically Authentic. Own That Damn Business

HOW WAS MY **SLEEP LAST NIGHT**

(1) (2) (3) (4) (5) (6) (7) (8) (9) (10)

HOW **MOTIVATED** DO I FEEL TODAY

(1) (2) (3) (4) (5) (6) (7) (8) (9) (10)

WHERE IS MY **PHYSICAL ENERGY LEVEL**

(1) (2) (3) (4) (5) (6) (7) (8) (9) (10)

HOW IS MY **EMOTIONAL CAPACITY**

(1) (2) (3) (4) (5) (6) (7) (8) (9) (10)

SHITTY ———————————————— AWESOME

THREE THINGS I'M
GRATEFUL FOR:

_____
_____
_____
_____
_____
_____
_____

REFLECTION OF YESTERDAY

DID I DO THE THINGS I **COMMITED** TO DO?   (Y) (N)

DID I DO SOMETHING FOR **MYSELF**? (joy, rest, movement, fun)   (Y) (N)

DID I PROTECT MY **ENERGY** AND SET **CLEAR BOUNDARIES**?   (Y) (N)

DID I **CELEBRATE** A SMALL WIN (or acknowledge progress)   (Y) (N)

DID I CHECK IN WITH MY **VISION + GOALS** (even briefly)?   (Y) (N)

DID I MAKE AT LEAST ONE **BOLD MOVE** OR **CEO DECISION**?   (Y) (N)

DID I **STAY FOCUSED** ON MY GROWTH?   (Y) (N)

IF I ANSWERED "NO" TO ANY
WHAT DO I SHIFT TODAY?

_____
_____
_____
_____
_____

3 ACTION STEPS (COMMITMENTS) I WILL DO TODAY
THINGS YOU WILL COMMIT TO YOURSELF AND YOUR BUSINESS TO SUPPORT YOUR VISION

SOMETHING I NEED TO **REMIND MYSELF** OF TODAY _____

BUSINESS TO DO LIST:

PERSONAL TO DO LIST:

TOP PRIORITIES TODAY

_____

_____

_____

_____

HOW MUCH **TIME** WILL I
DEDICATE TO MY BUSINESS
TODAY?

6 am

7 am

8 am

9 am

10 am

11 am

12 pm

1 pm

2 pm

3 pm

4 pm

5 pm

6 pm

7 pm

She's the STRATEGY

JAN FEB MAR APR MAY JUN JUL AUG SEP OCT NOV DEC 20___
1 2 3 4 5 6 7 8 9 10 11 12 13 14 15 16 17 18 19 20 21 22 23 24 25 26 27 28 29 30 31

HOW WAS MY SLEEP LAST NIGHT

1 2 3 4 5 6 7 8 9 10

HOW MOTIVATED DO I FEEL TODAY

1 2 3 4 5 6 7 8 9 10

WHERE IS MY PHYSICAL ENERGY LEVEL

1 2 3 4 5 6 7 8 9 10

HOW IS MY EMOTIONAL CAPACITY

1 2 3 4 5 6 7 8 9 10

SHITTY ————————————————— AWESOME

THREE THINGS I'M **GRATEFUL FOR:**

REFLECTION OF YESTERDAY

DID I DO THE THINGS I **COMMITED** TO DO?   Y N

DID I DO SOMETHING FOR **MYSELF**? (joy, rest, movement, fun)   Y N

DID I PROTECT MY **ENERGY** AND SET **CLEAR BOUNDARIES**?   Y N

DID I **CELEBRATE** A SMALL WIN (or acknowledge progress)   Y N

DID I CHECK IN WITH MY **VISION + GOALS** (even briefly)?   Y N

DID I MAKE AT LEAST ONE **BOLD MOVE** OR **CEO DECISION**?   Y N

DID I **STAY FOCUSED** ON MY GROWTH?   Y N

IF I ANSWERED "NO" TO ANY **WHAT DO I SHIFT TODAY**?

3 ACTION STEPS (COMMITMENTS) I WILL DO TODAY
THINGS YOU WILL COMMIT TO YOURSELF AND YOUR BUSINESS TO SUPPORT YOUR VISION

SOMETHING I NEED TO **REMIND MYSELF** OF TODAY _____

BUSINESS TO DO LIST:

PERSONAL TO DO LIST:

TOP PRIORITIES TODAY

_____

_____

_____

HOW MUCH **TIME** WILL I
DEDICATE TO MY BUSINESS
TODAY?

6 am

7 am

8 am

9 am

10 am

11 am

12 pm

1 pm

2 pm

3 pm

4 pm

5 pm

6 pm

7 pm

JAN   FEB   MAR   APR   MAY   JUN   JUL   AUG   SEP   OCT   NOV   DEC   20___
1 2 3 4 5 6 7 8 9 10 11 12 13 14 15 16 17 18 19 20 21 22 23 24 25 26 27 28 29 30 31

HOW WAS MY **SLEEP LAST NIGHT**

(1) (2) (3) (4) (5) (6) (7) (8) (9) (10)

HOW **MOTIVATED** DO I FEEL TODAY

(1) (2) (3) (4) (5) (6) (7) (8) (9) (10)

WHERE IS MY **PHYSICAL ENERGY LEVEL**

(1) (2) (3) (4) (5) (6) (7) (8) (9) (10)

HOW IS MY **EMOTIONAL CAPACITY**

(1) (2) (3) (4) (5) (6) (7) (8) (9) (10)

SHITTY ———————————————————— AWESOME

THREE THINGS I'M
GRATEFUL FOR:

_____
_____
_____
_____
_____
_____
_____

REFLECTION OF YESTERDAY

DID I DO THE THINGS I **COMMITED** TO DO?   (Y) (N)

DID I DO SOMETHING FOR **MYSELF**? (joy, rest, movement, fun)   (Y) (N)

DID I PROTECT MY **ENERGY** AND SET **CLEAR BOUNDARIES**?   (Y) (N)

DID I **CELEBRATE** A SMALL WIN (or acknowledge progress)   (Y) (N)

DID I CHECK IN WITH MY **VISION + GOALS** (even briefly)?   (Y) (N)

DID I MAKE AT LEAST ONE **BOLD MOVE** OR **CEO DECISION**?   (Y) (N)

DID I **STAY FOCUSED** ON MY GROWTH?   (Y) (N)

IF I ANSWERED "NO" TO ANY
WHAT DO I SHIFT TODAY?

_____
_____
_____
_____

---

3 ACTION STEPS (COMMITMENTS) I WILL DO TODAY
THINGS YOU WILL COMMIT TO YOURSELF AND YOUR BUSINESS TO SUPPORT YOUR VISION

SOMETHING I NEED TO **REMIND MYSELF** OF TODAY _____

BUSINESS TO DO LIST:

PERSONAL TO DO LIST:

TOP PRIORITIES TODAY

_____
_____
_____

HOW MUCH **TIME** WILL I DEDICATE TO MY BUSINESS TODAY?

6 am

7 am

8 am

9 am

10 am

11 am

12 pm

1 pm

2 pm

3 pm

4 pm

5 pm

6 pm

7 pm

MONTHLY CHECK-IN
A MOMENT TO ZOOM OUT, REALIGN, AND POWER UP.

MONTHLY WINS

MY **PROUDEST** MOMENT

A MILESTONE I **REACHED** (BIG OR SMALL):

A CHALLENGE I **OVERCAME**

BY THE NUMBERS

CLIENTS SERVED: _____

REVENUE/INCOME: _____

OFFERS PROMOTED/LAUNCHED: _____

PERSONAL REFLECTION

I FELT LIKE THE CEO OF MY LIFE   Ⓨ Ⓝ

I TOOK CARE OF MYSELF CONSISTENTLY   Ⓨ Ⓝ

I FELT ALIGNED WITH MY BUSINESS VISION: Ⓨ Ⓝ

WHAT DID I LEARN ABOUT MYSELF THIS MONTH? _____

WHAT DO I WANT TO CELEBRATE MORE OFTEN? _____

WHAT BELIEF OR HABIT NEEDS TO SHIFT NEXT MONTH? _____

RESET + RECOMMIT

WHAT WILL I TAKE WITH ME INTO NEXT MONTH?

WHAT WILL I LEAVE BEHIND WITH?

WHAT DO I WANT TO EXPERIENCE MORE OF?

MY **FOCUS THEME** FOR **NEXT MONTH**: _____

MONTHLY **GOAL PLANNER** LIKE A
DAMN BUSINESS BADASS

MY **MONTHLY** FOCUS

MONTH: _____

WHAT SPECIFIC OUTCOME DO I WANT TO CREATE BY THE END OF THIS MONTH?

MY **MEASURABLE** GOAL

(CLIENT COUNT, REVENUE TARGET, AUDIENCE GROWTH, ETC.) _____

_____

MY SUPPORT SYSTEM	**MY SELF-CARE STRATEGY**	**VISION BUILDER**
WHAT SUPPORT, TOOLS, OR PEOPLE DO I NEED TO HELP ME MOVE FORWARD?	WHAT WILL BALANCE, REST, OR JOY LOOK LIKE THIS MONTH?	WHO AM I BECOMING IN THIS BUSINESS?

QUARTER: Q1 / Q2 / Q3 / Q4 (CIRCLE ONE)   YEAR: _____

IF I FULLY TRUSTED MYSELF, WHAT WOULD I CREATE OR LAUNCH THIS QUARTER? _____

_____

WHAT DOES SUCCESS LOOK AND FEEL LIKE TO ME (NOT SOCIETY'S VERSION)? _____

_____

WHAT DO I WANT TO BE KNOWN FOR BY THE END OF THIS QUARTER?

_____

She's the
STRATEGY
Unapologetically Authentic. Own That Damn Business.

HOW WAS MY **SLEEP LAST NIGHT**

(1) (2) (3) (4) (5) (6) (7) (8) (9) (10)

HOW **MOTIVATED** DO I FEEL TODAY

(1) (2) (3) (4) (5) (6) (7) (8) (9) (10)

WHERE IS MY **PHYSICAL ENERGY LEVEL**

(1) (2) (3) (4) (5) (6) (7) (8) (9) (10)

HOW IS MY **EMOTIONAL CAPACITY**

(1) (2) (3) (4) (5) (6) (7) (8) (9) (10)

SHITTY ——————————————— AWESOME

THREE THINGS I'M **GRATEFUL FOR:**

_____

_____

_____

_____

_____

_____

REFLECTION OF YESTERDAY

DID I DO THE THINGS I **COMMITED** TO DO? (Y) (N)

DID I DO SOMETHING FOR **MYSELF**? (joy, rest, movement, fun) (Y) (N)

DID I PROTECT MY **ENERGY** AND SET **CLEAR BOUNDARIES**? (Y) (N)

DID I **CELEBRATE** A SMALL WIN (or acknowledge progress) (Y) (N)

DID I CHECK IN WITH MY **VISION + GOALS** (even briefly)? (Y) (N)

DID I MAKE AT LEAST ONE **BOLD MOVE** OR **CEO DECISION**? (Y) (N)

DID I **STAY FOCUSED** ON MY GROWTH? (Y) (N)

IF I ANSWERED "NO" TO ANY
WHAT DO I SHIFT TODAY?

_____

_____

_____

_____

_____

3 ACTION STEPS (COMMITMENTS) I WILL DO TODAY

THINGS YOU WILL COMMIT TO YOURSELF AND YOUR BUSINESS TO SUPPORT YOUR VISION

SOMETHING I NEED TO **REMIND MYSELF** OF TODAY _____

BUSINESS TO DO LIST:

PERSONAL TO DO LIST:

TOP PRIORITIES TODAY

_____

_____

_____

HOW MUCH **TIME** WILL I DEDICATE TO MY BUSINESS TODAY?

6 am

7 am

8 am

9 am

10 am

11 am

12 pm

1 pm

2 pm

3 pm

4 pm

5 pm

6 pm

7 pm

HOW WAS MY **SLEEP LAST NIGHT**

(1)(2)(3)(4)(5)(6)(7)(8)(9)(10)

HOW **MOTIVATED** DO I FEEL TODAY

(1)(2)(3)(4)(5)(6)(7)(8)(9)(10)

WHERE IS MY **PHYSICAL ENERGY LEVEL**

(1)(2)(3)(4)(5)(6)(7)(8)(9)(10)

HOW IS MY **EMOTIONAL CAPACITY**

(1)(2)(3)(4)(5)(6)(7)(8)(9)(10)

SHITTY ——————————————— AWESOME

THREE THINGS I'M **GRATEFUL FOR:**

_____
_____
_____
_____
_____
_____
_____

REFLECTION OF YESTERDAY

DID I DO THE THINGS I **COMMITED** TO DO? (Y)(N)

DID I DO SOMETHING FOR **MYSELF**? (joy, rest, movement, fun) (Y)(N)

DID I PROTECT MY **ENERGY** AND SET **CLEAR BOUNDARIES**? (Y)(N)

DID I **CELEBRATE** A SMALL WIN (or acknowledge progress) (Y)(N)

DID I CHECK IN WITH MY **VISION + GOALS** (even briefly)? (Y)(N)

DID I MAKE AT LEAST ONE **BOLD MOVE** OR **CEO DECISION**? (Y)(N)

DID I **STAY FOCUSED** ON MY GROWTH? (Y)(N)

IF I ANSWERED "NO" TO ANY **WHAT DO I SHIFT TODAY**?

_____
_____
_____
_____
_____

3 **ACTION STEPS** (COMMITMENTS) I WILL DO TODAY
THINGS YOU WILL COMMIT TO YOURSELF AND YOUR BUSINESS TO SUPPORT YOUR VISION

SOMETHING I NEED TO **REMIND MYSELF** OF TODAY _____

BUSINESS TO DO LIST:

PERSONAL TO DO LIST:

TOP PRIORITIES TODAY

_____

_____

_____

_____

HOW MUCH **TIME** WILL I
DEDICATE TO MY BUSINESS
TODAY?

6 am

7 am

8 am

9 am

10 am

11 am

12 pm

1 pm

2 pm

3 pm

4 pm

5 pm

6 pm

7 pm

She's the
STRATEGY
Unapologetically Authentic. Own That Damn Business.

JAN FEB MAR APR MAY JUN JUL AUG SEP OCT NOV DEC 20___
1 2 3 4 5 6 7 8 9 10 11 12 13 14 15 16 17 18 19 20 21 22 23 24 25 26 27 28 29 30 31

HOW WAS MY **SLEEP LAST NIGHT**

(1) (2) (3) (4) (5) (6) (7) (8) (9) (10)

HOW **MOTIVATED** DO I FEEL TODAY

(1) (2) (3) (4) (5) (6) (7) (8) (9) (10)

WHERE IS MY **PHYSICAL ENERGY LEVEL**

(1) (2) (3) (4) (5) (6) (7) (8) (9) (10)

HOW IS MY **EMOTIONAL CAPACITY**

(1) (2) (3) (4) (5) (6) (7) (8) (9) (10)

SHITTY ——————————————— AWESOME

THREE THINGS I'M
GRATEFUL FOR:

_____
_____
_____
_____
_____
_____
_____

REFLECTION OF YESTERDAY

DID I DO THE THINGS I **COMMITED** TO DO? (Y)(N)

DID I DO SOMETHING FOR **MYSELF**? (joy, rest, movement, fun) (Y)(N)

DID I PROTECT MY **ENERGY** AND SET **CLEAR BOUNDARIES**? (Y)(N)

DID I **CELEBRATE** A SMALL WIN (or acknowledge progress) (Y)(N)

DID I CHECK IN WITH MY **VISION + GOALS** (even briefly)? (Y)(N)

DID I MAKE AT LEAST ONE **BOLD MOVE** OR **CEO DECISION**? (Y)(N)

DID I **STAY FOCUSED** ON MY GROWTH? (Y)(N)

IF I ANSWERED "NO" TO ANY
WHAT DO I SHIFT TODAY?

_____
_____
_____
_____
_____

3 ACTION STEPS (COMMITMENTS) I WILL DO TODAY
THINGS YOU WILL COMMIT TO YOURSELF AND YOUR BUSINESS TO SUPPORT YOUR VISION

SOMETHING I NEED TO **REMIND MYSELF** OF TODAY _____

BUSINESS TO DO LIST:

PERSONAL TO DO LIST:

TOP PRIORITIES TODAY

HOW MUCH **TIME** WILL I
DEDICATE TO MY BUSINESS
TODAY?

6 am

7 am

8 am

9 am

10 am

11 am

12 pm

1 pm

2 pm

3 pm

4 pm

5 pm

6 pm

7 pm

HOW WAS MY **SLEEP LAST NIGHT**

(1) (2) (3) (4) (5) (6) (7) (8) (9) (10)

HOW **MOTIVATED** DO I FEEL TODAY

(1) (2) (3) (4) (5) (6) (7) (8) (9) (10)

WHERE IS MY **PHYSICAL ENERGY LEVEL**

(1) (2) (3) (4) (5) (6) (7) (8) (9) (10)

HOW IS MY **EMOTIONAL CAPACITY**

(1) (2) (3) (4) (5) (6) (7) (8) (9) (10)

SHITTY ————————————————— AWESOME

THREE THINGS I'M **GRATEFUL FOR:**

_____
_____
_____
_____
_____
_____
_____

REFLECTION OF YESTERDAY

DID I DO THE THINGS I **COMMITED** TO DO?   (Y) (N)

DID I DO SOMETHING FOR **MYSELF**? (joy, rest, movement, fun)   (Y) (N)

DID I PROTECT MY **ENERGY** AND SET **CLEAR BOUNDARIES**?   (Y) (N)

DID I **CELEBRATE** A SMALL WIN (or acknowledge progress)   (Y) (N)

DID I CHECK IN WITH MY **VISION + GOALS** (even briefly)?   (Y) (N)

DID I MAKE AT LEAST ONE **BOLD MOVE** OR **CEO DECISION**?   (Y) (N)

DID I **STAY FOCUSED** ON MY GROWTH?   (Y) (N)

IF I ANSWERED "NO" TO ANY **WHAT DO I SHIFT TODAY**?

_____
_____
_____
_____
_____

3 ACTION STEPS (COMMITMENTS) I WILL DO TODAY
THINGS YOU WILL COMMIT TO YOURSELF AND YOUR BUSINESS TO SUPPORT YOUR VISION

SOMETHING I NEED TO **REMIND MYSELF** OF TODAY _____

BUSINESS TO DO LIST:

PERSONAL TO DO LIST:

TOP PRIORITIES TODAY

_____

_____

_____

_____

HOW MUCH **TIME** WILL I DEDICATE TO MY BUSINESS TODAY?

6 am

7 am

8 am

9 am

10 am

11 am

12 pm

1 pm

2 pm

3 pm

4 pm

5 pm

6 pm

7 pm

HOW WAS MY **SLEEP LAST NIGHT**

(1) (2) (3) (4) (5) (6) (7) (8) (9) (10)

HOW **MOTIVATED** DO I FEEL TODAY

(1) (2) (3) (4) (5) (6) (7) (8) (9) (10)

WHERE IS MY **PHYSICAL ENERGY LEVEL**

(1) (2) (3) (4) (5) (6) (7) (8) (9) (10)

HOW IS MY **EMOTIONAL CAPACITY**

(1) (2) (3) (4) (5) (6) (7) (8) (9) (10)

SHITTY ——————————————————— AWESOME

THREE THINGS I'M **GRATEFUL FOR:**

_____

_____

_____

_____

_____

_____

_____

REFLECTION OF YESTERDAY

DID I DO THE THINGS I **COMMITED** TO DO?	(Y)(N)
DID I DO SOMETHING FOR **MYSELF**? (joy, rest, movement, fun)	(Y)(N)
DID I PROTECT MY **ENERGY** AND SET **CLEAR BOUNDARIES**?	(Y)(N)
DID I **CELEBRATE** A SMALL WIN (or acknowledge progress)	(Y)(N)
DID I CHECK IN WITH MY **VISION + GOALS** (even briefly)?	(Y)(N)
DID I MAKE AT LEAST ONE **BOLD MOVE** OR **CEO DECISION**?	(Y)(N)
DID I **STAY FOCUSED** ON MY GROWTH?	(Y)(N)

IF I ANSWERED "NO" TO ANY **WHAT DO I SHIFT TODAY**?

_____

_____

_____

_____

3 ACTION STEPS (COMMITMENTS) I WILL DO TODAY
THINGS YOU WILL COMMIT TO YOURSELF AND YOUR BUSINESS TO SUPPORT YOUR VISION

SOMETHING I NEED TO **REMIND MYSELF** OF TODAY _____

BUSINESS TO DO LIST:

PERSONAL TO DO LIST:

TOP PRIORITIES TODAY

_____

_____

_____

HOW MUCH **TIME** WILL I
DEDICATE TO MY BUSINESS
TODAY?

6 am

7 am

8 am

9 am

10 am

11 am

12 pm

1 pm

2 pm

3 pm

4 pm

5 pm

6 pm

7 pm

She's the
STRATEGY
Unapologetically Authentic. Own That Damn Business.

HOW WAS MY **SLEEP LAST NIGHT**

① ② ③ ④ ⑤ ⑥ ⑦ ⑧ ⑨ ⑩

HOW **MOTIVATED** DO I FEEL TODAY

① ② ③ ④ ⑤ ⑥ ⑦ ⑧ ⑨ ⑩

WHERE IS MY **PHYSICAL ENERGY LEVEL**

① ② ③ ④ ⑤ ⑥ ⑦ ⑧ ⑨ ⑩

HOW IS MY **EMOTIONAL CAPACITY**

① ② ③ ④ ⑤ ⑥ ⑦ ⑧ ⑨ ⑩

SHITTY ———————————————— AWESOME

THREE THINGS I'M **GRATEFUL FOR:**

_____
_____
_____
_____
_____
_____

REFLECTION OF YESTERDAY

DID I DO THE THINGS I **COMMITED** TO DO?   Ⓨ Ⓝ

DID I DO SOMETHING FOR **MYSELF**? (joy, rest, movement, fun)   Ⓨ Ⓝ

DID I PROTECT MY **ENERGY** AND SET **CLEAR BOUNDARIES**?   Ⓨ Ⓝ

DID I **CELEBRATE** A SMALL WIN (or acknowledge progress)   Ⓨ Ⓝ

DID I CHECK IN WITH MY **VISION + GOALS** (even briefly)?   Ⓨ Ⓝ

DID I MAKE AT LEAST ONE **BOLD MOVE** OR **CEO DECISION**?   Ⓨ Ⓝ

DID I **STAY FOCUSED** ON MY GROWTH?   Ⓨ Ⓝ

IF I ANSWERED "NO" TO ANY **WHAT DO I SHIFT TODAY**?

_____
_____
_____
_____

3 ACTION STEPS (COMMITMENTS) I WILL DO TODAY
THINGS YOU WILL COMMIT TO YOURSELF AND YOUR BUSINESS TO SUPPORT YOUR VISION

SOMETHING I NEED TO **REMIND MYSELF** OF TODAY _____

BUSINESS TO DO LIST:

PERSONAL TO DO LIST:

TOP PRIORITIES TODAY

_____

_____

_____

_____

HOW MUCH **TIME** WILL I
DEDICATE TO MY BUSINESS
TODAY?

6 am

7 am

8 am

9 am

10 am

11 am

12 pm

1 pm

2 pm

3 pm

4 pm

5 pm

6 pm

7 pm

HOW WAS MY **SLEEP LAST NIGHT**

(1) (2) (3) (4) (5) (6) (7) (8) (9) (10)

HOW **MOTIVATED** DO I FEEL TODAY

(1) (2) (3) (4) (5) (6) (7) (8) (9) (10)

WHERE IS MY **PHYSICAL ENERGY LEVEL**

(1) (2) (3) (4) (5) (6) (7) (8) (9) (10)

HOW IS MY **EMOTIONAL CAPACITY**

(1) (2) (3) (4) (5) (6) (7) (8) (9) (10)

SHITTY ——————————————————— AWESOME

THREE THINGS I'M
GRATEFUL FOR:

_____
_____
_____
_____
_____
_____
_____

REFLECTION OF YESTERDAY

DID I DO THE THINGS I **COMMITED** TO DO?   (Y) (N)

DID I DO SOMETHING FOR **MYSELF**? (joy, rest, movement, fun)   (Y) (N)

DID I PROTECT MY **ENERGY** AND SET **CLEAR BOUNDARIES**?   (Y) (N)

DID I **CELEBRATE** A SMALL WIN (or acknowledge progress)   (Y) (N)

DID I CHECK IN WITH MY **VISION + GOALS** (even briefly)?   (Y) (N)

DID I MAKE AT LEAST ONE **BOLD MOVE** OR **CEO DECISION**?   (Y) (N)

DID I **STAY FOCUSED** ON MY GROWTH?   (Y) (N)

IF I ANSWERED "NO" TO ANY
WHAT DO I SHIFT TODAY?

_____
_____
_____
_____

3 ACTION STEPS (COMMITMENTS) I WILL DO TODAY
THINGS YOU WILL COMMIT TO YOURSELF AND YOUR BUSINESS TO SUPPORT YOUR VISION

SOMETHING I NEED TO **REMIND MYSELF** OF TODAY _____

BUSINESS TO DO LIST:

PERSONAL TO DO LIST:

TOP PRIORITIES TODAY

_____

_____

_____

_____

HOW MUCH **TIME** WILL I
DEDICATE TO MY BUSINESS
TODAY?

6 am

7 am

8 am

9 am

10 am

11 am

12 pm

1 pm

2 pm

3 pm

4 pm

5 pm

6 pm

7 pm

WEEKLY CHECK-IN

PERSONAL ENERGY & WELL-BEING
On a scale of 1–10, how would I rate...

MY OVERALL **ENERGY** THIS WEEK
① ② ③ ④ ⑤ ⑥ ⑦ ⑧ ⑨ ⑩

MY **EMOTIONAL CAPACITY** THIS WEEK
① ② ③ ④ ⑤ ⑥ ⑦ ⑧ ⑨ ⑩

MY **MOTIVATION + CLARITY** THIS WEEK
① ② ③ ④ ⑤ ⑥ ⑦ ⑧ ⑨ ⑩

SHITTY ———————————————— AWESOME

WHAT SUPPORTED MY WELL-BEING THIS WEEK?

WHAT DRAINED ME THAT I WANT TO SHIFT OR ELIMINATE?

WHAT DID I DO JUST FOR ME THIS WEEK?

BUSINESS & LEADERSHIP REFLECTIONS

DID I **STAY FOCUSED** ON MY TOP PRIORITIES? Ⓨ Ⓝ

DID I **LEAD** WITH CONFIDENCE, EVEN WHEN IT WAS HARD? Ⓨ Ⓝ

DID I **SHOW UP** FOR MY BRAND IN A WAY I'M PROUD OF? Ⓨ Ⓝ

DID I COMMUNICATE **CLEAR BOUNDARIES** AROUND MY TIME? Ⓨ Ⓝ

WHAT WORKED REALLY WELL IN MY BUSINESS THIS WEEK?

WHAT CHALLENGES CAME UP, AND WHAT DID I LEARN FROM THEM?

WHAT BOLD MOVE DID I MAKE (OR WISH I HAD)?

ALIGNMENT & INTENTION

AM I STILL MOVING TOWARD MY BIGGER VISION — OR AM I JUST STAYING BUSY?

WHAT DO I NEED TO PAUSE, PIVOT, OR RELEASE RIGHT NOW?

WHAT'S ONE THING I WANT TO RECOMMIT TO NEXT WEEK?

NEXT WEEK'S FOCUS

ONE BOLD THING I'LL DO THIS WEEK

ONE BOUNDARY I'LL PROTECT

WEEKLY **GOAL PLANNER** LIKE A
DAMN BUSINESS BADASS

MY **WEEKLY** FOCUS
TOP 3 POWER GOALS FOR THIS WEEK - (WHAT ACTUALLY MOVES THE NEEDLE — NOT BUSY WORK.)

ENERGY + MINDSET FOCUS:

(ONE VIBE, MANTRA, OR ENERGY YOU'RE CHOOSING TO LEAD WITH THIS WEEK.) ....

CELEBRATE YOUR DAMN WINS:

INNER WINS **(MINDSET + ENERGY)** THE MOMENTS YOU CHOSE GROWTH, CALM, COURAGE, OR CLARITY OVER CHAOS.	**ACTION WINS** **(SH*T YOU ACTUALLY DID)** TANGIBLE MOVES YOU MADE — BIG OR SMALL — THAT PROVE YOU'RE BUILDING MOMENTUM.	**ALIGNMENT WINS** **(SOUL-LEVEL YES MOMENTS)** WHEN SOMETHING FELT RIGHT, EASY, ALIGNED, OR JOYFULLY YOU.

WHAT NEEDS TO **SHIFT** ASAP?

HOW WAS MY **SLEEP LAST NIGHT**

① ② ③ ④ ⑤ ⑥ ⑦ ⑧ ⑨ ⑩

HOW **MOTIVATED** DO I FEEL TODAY

① ② ③ ④ ⑤ ⑥ ⑦ ⑧ ⑨ ⑩

WHERE IS MY **PHYSICAL ENERGY LEVEL**

① ② ③ ④ ⑤ ⑥ ⑦ ⑧ ⑨ ⑩

HOW IS MY **EMOTIONAL CAPACITY**

① ② ③ ④ ⑤ ⑥ ⑦ ⑧ ⑨ ⑩

SHITTY ———————————————————— AWESOME

THREE THINGS I'M **GRATEFUL FOR:**

_____
_____
_____
_____
_____
_____
_____
_____

REFLECTION OF YESTERDAY

DID I DO THE THINGS I **COMMITED** TO DO?	Y	N
DID I DO SOMETHING FOR **MYSELF**? (joy, rest, movement, fun)	Y	N
DID I PROTECT MY **ENERGY** AND SET **CLEAR BOUNDARIES**?	Y	N
DID I **CELEBRATE** A SMALL WIN (or acknowledge progress)	Y	N
DID I CHECK IN WITH MY **VISION + GOALS** (even briefly)?	Y	N
DID I MAKE AT LEAST ONE **BOLD MOVE** OR **CEO DECISION**?	Y	N
DID I **STAY FOCUSED** ON MY GROWTH?	Y	N

IF I ANSWERED "NO" TO ANY
WHAT DO I SHIFT TODAY?

_____
_____
_____
_____
_____

3 ACTION STEPS (COMMITMENTS) I WILL DO TODAY
THINGS YOU WILL COMMIT TO YOURSELF AND YOUR BUSINESS TO SUPPORT YOUR VISION

SOMETHING I NEED TO **REMIND MYSELF** OF TODAY _____

BUSINESS TO DO LIST:

PERSONAL TO DO LIST:

TOP PRIORITIES TODAY

_____

_____

_____

HOW MUCH **TIME** WILL I DEDICATE TO MY BUSINESS TODAY?

6 am

7 am

8 am

9 am

10 am

11 am

12 pm

1 pm

2 pm

3 pm

4 pm

5 pm

6 pm

7 pm

She's the STRATEGY
Unapologetically Authentic. Own That Damn Business

HOW WAS MY **SLEEP LAST NIGHT**

(1)(2)(3)(4)(5)(6)(7)(8)(9)(10)

HOW **MOTIVATED** DO I FEEL TODAY

(1)(2)(3)(4)(5)(6)(7)(8)(9)(10)

WHERE IS MY **PHYSICAL ENERGY LEVEL**

(1)(2)(3)(4)(5)(6)(7)(8)(9)(10)

HOW IS MY **EMOTIONAL CAPACITY**

(1)(2)(3)(4)(5)(6)(7)(8)(9)(10)

SHITTY ——————————————— AWESOME

THREE THINGS I'M
GRATEFUL FOR:

_____
_____
_____
_____
_____
_____
_____

REFLECTION OF YESTERDAY

DID I DO THE THINGS I **COMMITED** TO DO?	(Y)(N)	
DID I DO SOMETHING FOR **MYSELF**? (joy, rest, movement, fun)	(Y)(N)	
DID I PROTECT MY **ENERGY** AND SET **CLEAR BOUNDARIES**?	(Y)(N)	
DID I **CELEBRATE** A SMALL WIN (or acknowledge progress)	(Y)(N)	
DID I CHECK IN WITH MY **VISION + GOALS** (even briefly)?	(Y)(N)	
DID I MAKE AT LEAST ONE **BOLD MOVE** OR **CEO DECISION**?	(Y)(N)	
DID I **STAY FOCUSED** ON MY GROWTH?	(Y)(N)	

IF I ANSWERED "NO" TO ANY
WHAT DO I SHIFT TODAY?

_____
_____
_____
_____
_____

3 ACTION STEPS (COMMITMENTS) I WILL DO TODAY
THINGS YOU WILL COMMIT TO YOURSELF AND YOUR BUSINESS TO SUPPORT YOUR VISION

SOMETHING I NEED TO **REMIND MYSELF** OF TODAY _____

BUSINESS TO DO LIST:

PERSONAL TO DO LIST:

TOP PRIORITIES TODAY

_____

_____

_____

_____

HOW MUCH **TIME** WILL I DEDICATE TO MY BUSINESS TODAY?

6 am _____ ✓

7 am _____ ✓

8 am _____ ✓

9 am _____ ✓

10 am _____ ✓

11 am _____ ✓

12 pm _____ ✓

1 pm _____ ✓

2 pm _____ ✓

3 pm _____ ✓

4 pm _____ ✓

5 pm _____ ✓

6 pm _____ ✓

7 pm _____ ✓

She's the STRATEGY
Unapologetically Authentic. Own That Damn Business

JAN   FEB   MAR   APR   MAY   JUN   JUL   AUG   SEP   OCT   NOV   DEC   20___
1 2 3 4 5 6 7 8 9 10 11 12 13 14 15 16 17 18 19 20 21 22 23 24 25 26 27 28 29 30 31

HOW WAS MY **SLEEP LAST NIGHT**
① ② ③ ④ ⑤ ⑥ ⑦ ⑧ ⑨ ⑩

HOW **MOTIVATED** DO I FEEL TODAY
① ② ③ ④ ⑤ ⑥ ⑦ ⑧ ⑨ ⑩

WHERE IS MY **PHYSICAL ENERGY LEVEL**
① ② ③ ④ ⑤ ⑥ ⑦ ⑧ ⑨ ⑩

HOW IS MY **EMOTIONAL CAPACITY**
① ② ③ ④ ⑤ ⑥ ⑦ ⑧ ⑨ ⑩

SHITTY ——————————————— AWESOME

THREE THINGS I'M **GRATEFUL FOR:**

_____
_____
_____
_____
_____
_____
_____

REFLECTION OF YESTERDAY

DID I DO THE THINGS I **COMMITED** TO DO?   Ⓨ Ⓝ

DID I DO SOMETHING FOR **MYSELF**? (joy, rest, movement, fun)   Ⓨ Ⓝ

DID I PROTECT MY **ENERGY** AND SET **CLEAR BOUNDARIES**?   Ⓨ Ⓝ

DID I **CELEBRATE** A SMALL WIN (or acknowledge progress)   Ⓨ Ⓝ

DID I CHECK IN WITH MY **VISION + GOALS** (even briefly)?   Ⓨ Ⓝ

DID I MAKE AT LEAST ONE **BOLD MOVE** OR **CEO DECISION**?   Ⓨ Ⓝ

DID I **STAY FOCUSED** ON MY GROWTH?   Ⓨ Ⓝ

IF I ANSWERED "NO" TO ANY
WHAT DO I SHIFT TODAY?

_____
_____
_____
_____
_____

3 **ACTION STEPS** (COMMITMENTS) I WILL DO TODAY
THINGS YOU WILL COMMIT TO YOURSELF AND YOUR BUSINESS TO SUPPORT YOUR VISION

SOMETHING I NEED TO **REMIND MYSELF** OF TODAY _____

BUSINESS TO DO LIST:

PERSONAL TO DO LIST:

TOP PRIORITIES TODAY

_____

_____

_____

HOW MUCH **TIME** WILL I
DEDICATE TO MY BUSINESS
TODAY?

6 am

7 am

8 am

9 am

10 am

11 am

12 pm

1 pm

2 pm

3 pm

4 pm

5 pm

6 pm

7 pm

HOW WAS MY **SLEEP LAST NIGHT**

① ② ③ ④ ⑤ ⑥ ⑦ ⑧ ⑨ ⑩

HOW **MOTIVATED** DO I FEEL TODAY

① ② ③ ④ ⑤ ⑥ ⑦ ⑧ ⑨ ⑩

WHERE IS MY **PHYSICAL ENERGY LEVEL**

① ② ③ ④ ⑤ ⑥ ⑦ ⑧ ⑨ ⑩

HOW IS MY **EMOTIONAL CAPACITY**

① ② ③ ④ ⑤ ⑥ ⑦ ⑧ ⑨ ⑩

SHITTY ————————————————— AWESOME

THREE THINGS I'M **GRATEFUL FOR:**

_____
_____
_____
_____
_____
_____
_____

REFLECTION OF YESTERDAY

DID I DO THE THINGS I **COMMITED** TO DO? Ⓨ Ⓝ

DID I DO SOMETHING FOR **MYSELF**? (joy, rest, movement, fun) Ⓨ Ⓝ

DID I PROTECT MY **ENERGY** AND SET **CLEAR BOUNDARIES**? Ⓨ Ⓝ

DID I **CELEBRATE** A SMALL WIN (or acknowledge progress) Ⓨ Ⓝ

DID I CHECK IN WITH MY **VISION + GOALS** (even briefly)? Ⓨ Ⓝ

DID I MAKE AT LEAST ONE **BOLD MOVE** OR **CEO DECISION**? Ⓨ Ⓝ

DID I **STAY FOCUSED** ON MY GROWTH? Ⓨ Ⓝ

IF I ANSWERED "NO" TO ANY **WHAT DO I SHIFT TODAY**?

_____
_____
_____
_____
_____

3 ACTION STEPS (COMMITMENTS) I WILL DO TODAY
THINGS YOU WILL COMMIT TO YOURSELF AND YOUR BUSINESS TO SUPPORT YOUR VISION

SOMETHING I NEED TO **REMIND MYSELF** OF TODAY _____

BUSINESS TO DO LIST:

PERSONAL TO DO LIST:

TOP PRIORITIES TODAY

_____

_____

_____

HOW MUCH **TIME** WILL I DEDICATE TO MY BUSINESS TODAY?

6 am

7 am

8 am

9 am

10 am

11 am

12 pm

1 pm

2 pm

3 pm

4 pm

5 pm

6 pm

7 pm

HOW WAS MY **SLEEP LAST NIGHT**

(1) (2) (3) (4) (5) (6) (7) (8) (9) (10)

HOW **MOTIVATED** DO I FEEL TODAY

(1) (2) (3) (4) (5) (6) (7) (8) (9) (10)

WHERE IS MY **PHYSICAL ENERGY LEVEL**

(1) (2) (3) (4) (5) (6) (7) (8) (9) (10)

HOW IS MY **EMOTIONAL CAPACITY**

(1) (2) (3) (4) (5) (6) (7) (8) (9) (10)

SHITTY ————————————————— AWESOME

THREE THINGS I'M
GRATEFUL FOR:

_____
_____
_____
_____
_____
_____
_____

REFLECTION OF YESTERDAY

DID I DO THE THINGS I **COMMITED** TO DO? (Y)(N)

DID I DO SOMETHING FOR **MYSELF**? (joy, rest, movement, fun) (Y)(N)

DID I PROTECT MY **ENERGY** AND SET **CLEAR BOUNDARIES**? (Y)(N)

DID I **CELEBRATE** A SMALL WIN (or acknowledge progress) (Y)(N)

DID I CHECK IN WITH MY **VISION + GOALS** (even briefly)? (Y)(N)

DID I MAKE AT LEAST ONE **BOLD MOVE** OR **CEO DECISION**? (Y)(N)

DID I **STAY FOCUSED** ON MY GROWTH? (Y)(N)

IF I ANSWERED "NO" TO ANY
WHAT DO I SHIFT TODAY?

_____
_____
_____
_____
_____

3 ACTION STEPS (COMMITMENTS) I WILL DO TODAY
THINGS YOU WILL COMMIT TO YOURSELF AND YOUR BUSINESS TO SUPPORT YOUR VISION

SOMETHING I NEED TO **REMIND MYSELF** OF TODAY _____

BUSINESS TO DO LIST:

PERSONAL TO DO LIST:

TOP PRIORITIES TODAY

_____

_____

_____

HOW MUCH **TIME** WILL I DEDICATE TO MY BUSINESS TODAY?

6 am

7 am

8 am

9 am

10 am

11 am

12 pm

1 pm

2 pm

3 pm

4 pm

5 pm

6 pm

7 pm

HOW WAS MY **SLEEP LAST NIGHT**

①②③④⑤⑥⑦⑧⑨⑩

HOW **MOTIVATED** DO I FEEL TODAY

①②③④⑤⑥⑦⑧⑨⑩

WHERE IS MY **PHYSICAL ENERGY LEVEL**

①②③④⑤⑥⑦⑧⑨⑩

HOW IS MY **EMOTIONAL CAPACITY**

①②③④⑤⑥⑦⑧⑨⑩

SHITTY ——————————————— AWESOME

THREE THINGS I'M **GRATEFUL FOR:**

_____
_____
_____
_____
_____
_____
_____

REFLECTION OF YESTERDAY

DID I DO THE THINGS I **COMMITED** TO DO? Ⓨ Ⓝ

DID I DO SOMETHING FOR **MYSELF**? (joy, rest, movement, fun) Ⓨ Ⓝ

DID I PROTECT MY **ENERGY** AND SET **CLEAR BOUNDARIES**? Ⓨ Ⓝ

DID I **CELEBRATE** A SMALL WIN (or acknowledge progress) Ⓨ Ⓝ

DID I CHECK IN WITH MY **VISION + GOALS** (even briefly)? Ⓨ Ⓝ

DID I MAKE AT LEAST ONE **BOLD MOVE** OR **CEO DECISION**? Ⓨ Ⓝ

DID I **STAY FOCUSED** ON MY GROWTH? Ⓨ Ⓝ

IF I ANSWERED "NO" TO ANY **WHAT DO I SHIFT TODAY**?

_____
_____
_____
_____
_____

3 **ACTION STEPS** (COMMITMENTS) I WILL DO TODAY
THINGS YOU WILL COMMIT TO YOURSELF AND YOUR BUSINESS TO SUPPORT YOUR VISION

SOMETHING I NEED TO **REMIND MYSELF** OF TODAY _____

BUSINESS TO DO LIST:

PERSONAL TO DO LIST:

TOP PRIORITIES TODAY

_____

_____

_____

HOW MUCH **TIME** WILL I DEDICATE TO MY BUSINESS TODAY?

6 am

7 am

8 am

9 am

10 am

11 am

12 pm

1 pm

2 pm

3 pm

4 pm

5 pm

6 pm

7 pm

HOW WAS MY **SLEEP LAST NIGHT**

(1) (2) (3) (4) (5) (6) (7) (8) (9) (10)

HOW **MOTIVATED** DO I FEEL TODAY

(1) (2) (3) (4) (5) (6) (7) (8) (9) (10)

WHERE IS MY **PHYSICAL ENERGY LEVEL**

(1) (2) (3) (4) (5) (6) (7) (8) (9) (10)

HOW IS MY **EMOTIONAL CAPACITY**

(1) (2) (3) (4) (5) (6) (7) (8) (9) (10)

SHITTY ———————————————————— AWESOME

THREE THINGS I'M **GRATEFUL FOR:**

_____

_____

_____

_____

_____

_____

REFLECTION OF YESTERDAY

DID I DO THE THINGS I **COMMITED** TO DO?	(Y) (N)	
DID I DO SOMETHING FOR **MYSELF**? (joy, rest, movement, fun)	(Y) (N)	
DID I PROTECT MY **ENERGY** AND SET **CLEAR BOUNDARIES**?	(Y) (N)	
DID I **CELEBRATE** A SMALL WIN (or acknowledge progress)	(Y) (N)	
DID I CHECK IN WITH MY **VISION + GOALS** (even briefly)?	(Y) (N)	
DID I MAKE AT LEAST ONE **BOLD MOVE** OR **CEO DECISION**?	(Y) (N)	
DID I **STAY FOCUSED** ON MY GROWTH?	(Y) (N)	

IF I ANSWERED "NO" TO ANY **WHAT DO I SHIFT TODAY**?

_____

_____

_____

_____

3 ACTION STEPS (COMMITMENTS) I WILL DO TODAY

THINGS YOU WILL COMMIT TO YOURSELF AND YOUR BUSINESS TO SUPPORT YOUR VISION

SOMETHING I NEED TO **REMIND MYSELF** OF TODAY _____

BUSINESS TO DO LIST:

PERSONAL TO DO LIST:

TOP PRIORITIES TODAY

_____

_____

_____

HOW MUCH **TIME** WILL I DEDICATE TO MY BUSINESS TODAY?

6 am

7 am

8 am

9 am

10 am

11 am

12 pm

1 pm

2 pm

3 pm

4 pm

5 pm

6 pm

7 pm

WEEKLY CHECK-IN

PERSONAL ENERGY & WELL-BEING
On a scale of 1–10, how would I rate...

MY OVERALL **ENERGY** THIS WEEK

(1) (2) (3) (4) (5) (6) (7) (8) (9) (10)

MY **EMOTIONAL CAPACITY** THIS WEEK

(1) (2) (3) (4) (5) (6) (7) (8) (9) (10)

MY **MOTIVATION + CLARITY** THIS WEEK

(1) (2) (3) (4) (5) (6) (7) (8) (9) (10)

SHITTY ———————————————— AWESOME

WHAT SUPPORTED MY WELL-BEING THIS WEEK?

WHAT DRAINED ME THAT I WANT TO SHIFT OR ELIMINATE?

WHAT DID I DO JUST FOR ME THIS WEEK?

BUSINESS & LEADERSHIP REFLECTIONS

DID I **STAY FOCUSED** ON MY TOP PRIORITIES? (Y) (N)

DID I **LEAD** WITH CONFIDENCE, EVEN WHEN IT WAS HARD? (Y) (N)

DID I **SHOW UP** FOR MY BRAND IN A WAY I'M PROUD OF? (Y) (N)

DID I COMMUNICATE **CLEAR BOUNDARIES** AROUND MY TIME? (Y) (N)

WHAT WORKED REALLY WELL IN MY BUSINESS THIS WEEK?

WHAT CHALLENGES CAME UP, AND WHAT DID I LEARN FROM THEM?

WHAT BOLD MOVE DID I MAKE (OR WISH I HAD)?

ALIGNMENT & INTENTION

AM I STILL MOVING TOWARD MY BIGGER VISION — OR AM I JUST STAYING BUSY?

WHAT DO I NEED TO PAUSE, PIVOT, OR RELEASE RIGHT NOW?

WHAT'S ONE THING I WANT TO RECOMMIT TO NEXT WEEK?

NEXT WEEK'S FOCUS

ONE BOLD THING I'LL DO THIS WEEK

ONE BOUNDARY I'LL PROTECT

WEEKLY **GOAL PLANNER** LIKE A
DAMN BUSINESS BADASS

MY **WEEKLY** FOCUS
TOP 3 POWER GOALS FOR THIS WEEK - (WHAT ACTUALLY MOVES THE NEEDLE — NOT BUSY WORK.)

ENERGY + MINDSET FOCUS:

(ONE VIBE, MANTRA, OR ENERGY YOU'RE CHOOSING TO LEAD WITH THIS WEEK.)

CELEBRATE YOUR DAMN WINS:

INNER WINS **(MINDSET + ENERGY)** THE MOMENTS YOU CHOSE GROWTH, CALM, COURAGE, OR CLARITY OVER CHAOS.	**ACTION WINS** **(SH*T YOU ACTUALLY DID)** TANGIBLE MOVES YOU MADE — BIG OR SMALL — THAT PROVE YOU'RE BUILDING MOMENTUM.	**ALIGNMENT WINS** **(SOUL-LEVEL YES MOMENTS)** WHEN SOMETHING FELT RIGHT, EASY, ALIGNED, OR JOYFULLY YOU.

WHAT NEEDS TO **SHIFT** ASAP?

HOW WAS MY **SLEEP LAST NIGHT**

(1) (2) (3) (4) (5) (6) (7) (8) (9) (10)

HOW **MOTIVATED** DO I FEEL TODAY

(1) (2) (3) (4) (5) (6) (7) (8) (9) (10)

WHERE IS MY **PHYSICAL ENERGY LEVEL**

(1) (2) (3) (4) (5) (6) (7) (8) (9) (10)

HOW IS MY **EMOTIONAL CAPACITY**

(1) (2) (3) (4) (5) (6) (7) (8) (9) (10)

SHITTY ——————————————————— AWESOME

THREE THINGS I'M
GRATEFUL FOR:

_____
_____
_____
_____
_____
_____
_____

REFLECTION OF YESTERDAY

DID I DO THE THINGS I **COMMITED** TO DO? (Y) (N)

DID I DO SOMETHING FOR **MYSELF**? (joy, rest, movement, fun) (Y) (N)

DID I PROTECT MY **ENERGY** AND SET **CLEAR BOUNDARIES**? (Y) (N)

DID I **CELEBRATE** A SMALL WIN (or acknowledge progress) (Y) (N)

DID I CHECK IN WITH MY **VISION + GOALS** (even briefly)? (Y) (N)

DID I MAKE AT LEAST ONE **BOLD MOVE** OR **CEO DECISION**? (Y) (N)

DID I **STAY FOCUSED** ON MY GROWTH? (Y) (N)

IF I ANSWERED "NO" TO ANY
WHAT DO I SHIFT TODAY?

_____
_____
_____
_____
_____

---

3 ACTION STEPS (COMMITMENTS) I WILL DO TODAY
THINGS YOU WILL COMMIT TO YOURSELF AND YOUR BUSINESS TO SUPPORT YOUR VISION

SOMETHING I NEED TO **REMIND MYSELF** OF TODAY _____

BUSINESS TO DO LIST:

PERSONAL TO DO LIST:

TOP PRIORITIES TODAY

_____

_____

_____

HOW MUCH **TIME** WILL I DEDICATE TO MY BUSINESS TODAY?

6 am

7 am

8 am

9 am

10 am

11 am

12 pm

1 pm

2 pm

3 pm

4 pm

5 pm

6 pm

7 pm

HOW WAS MY **SLEEP LAST NIGHT**

1 2 3 4 5 6 7 8 9 10

HOW **MOTIVATED** DO I FEEL TODAY

1 2 3 4 5 6 7 8 9 10

WHERE IS MY **PHYSICAL ENERGY LEVEL**

1 2 3 4 5 6 7 8 9 10

HOW IS MY **EMOTIONAL CAPACITY**

1 2 3 4 5 6 7 8 9 10

SHITTY ———————————————— AWESOME

THREE THINGS I'M **GRATEFUL FOR:**

_____
_____
_____
_____
_____
_____

REFLECTION OF YESTERDAY

DID I DO THE THINGS I **COMMITED** TO DO?   Y N

DID I DO SOMETHING FOR **MYSELF**? (joy, rest, movement, fun)   Y N

DID I PROTECT MY **ENERGY** AND SET **CLEAR BOUNDARIES**?   Y N

DID I **CELEBRATE** A SMALL WIN (or acknowledge progress)   Y N

DID I CHECK IN WITH MY **VISION + GOALS** (even briefly)?   Y N

DID I MAKE AT LEAST ONE **BOLD MOVE** OR **CEO DECISION**?   Y N

DID I **STAY FOCUSED** ON MY GROWTH?   Y N

IF I ANSWERED "NO" TO ANY **WHAT DO I SHIFT TODAY**?

_____
_____
_____
_____
_____

3 ACTION STEPS (COMMITMENTS) I WILL DO TODAY

THINGS YOU WILL COMMIT TO YOURSELF AND YOUR BUSINESS TO SUPPORT YOUR VISION

SOMETHING I NEED TO **REMIND MYSELF** OF TODAY _____

BUSINESS TO DO LIST:

PERSONAL TO DO LIST:

TOP PRIORITIES TODAY

_____

_____

_____

HOW MUCH **TIME** WILL I
DEDICATE TO MY BUSINESS
TODAY?

6 am

7 am

8 am

9 am

10 am

11 am

12 pm

1 pm

2 pm

3 pm

4 pm

5 pm

6 pm

7 pm

HOW WAS MY **SLEEP LAST NIGHT**

① ② ③ ④ ⑤ ⑥ ⑦ ⑧ ⑨ ⑩

HOW **MOTIVATED** DO I FEEL TODAY

① ② ③ ④ ⑤ ⑥ ⑦ ⑧ ⑨ ⑩

WHERE IS MY **PHYSICAL ENERGY LEVEL**

① ② ③ ④ ⑤ ⑥ ⑦ ⑧ ⑨ ⑩

HOW IS MY **EMOTIONAL CAPACITY**

① ② ③ ④ ⑤ ⑥ ⑦ ⑧ ⑨ ⑩

SHITTY ————————————————— AWESOME

THREE THINGS I'M **GRATEFUL FOR:**

_____
_____
_____
_____
_____
_____
_____
_____

REFLECTION OF YESTERDAY

DID I DO THE THINGS I **COMMITED** TO DO?   Ⓨ Ⓝ

DID I DO SOMETHING FOR **MYSELF**? (joy, rest, movement, fun)   Ⓨ Ⓝ

DID I PROTECT MY **ENERGY** AND SET **CLEAR BOUNDARIES**?   Ⓨ Ⓝ

DID I **CELEBRATE** A SMALL WIN (or acknowledge progress)   Ⓨ Ⓝ

DID I CHECK IN WITH MY **VISION + GOALS** (even briefly)?   Ⓨ Ⓝ

DID I MAKE AT LEAST ONE **BOLD MOVE** OR **CEO DECISION**?   Ⓨ Ⓝ

DID I **STAY FOCUSED** ON MY GROWTH?   Ⓨ Ⓝ

IF I ANSWERED "NO" TO ANY **WHAT DO I SHIFT TODAY**?

_____
_____
_____
_____
_____

3 ACTION STEPS (COMMITMENTS) I WILL DO TODAY
THINGS YOU WILL COMMIT TO YOURSELF AND YOUR BUSINESS TO SUPPORT YOUR VISION

SOMETHING I NEED TO **REMIND MYSELF** OF TODAY _____

BUSINESS TO DO LIST:

PERSONAL TO DO LIST:

TOP PRIORITIES TODAY

_____

_____

_____

HOW MUCH **TIME** WILL I
DEDICATE TO MY BUSINESS
TODAY?

6 am

7 am

8 am

9 am

10 am

11 am

12 pm

1 pm

2 pm

3 pm

4 pm

5 pm

6 pm

7 pm

HOW WAS MY **SLEEP LAST NIGHT**

(1)(2)(3)(4)(5)(6)(7)(8)(9)(10)

HOW **MOTIVATED** DO I FEEL TODAY

(1)(2)(3)(4)(5)(6)(7)(8)(9)(10)

WHERE IS MY **PHYSICAL ENERGY LEVEL**

(1)(2)(3)(4)(5)(6)(7)(8)(9)(10)

HOW IS MY **EMOTIONAL CAPACITY**

(1)(2)(3)(4)(5)(6)(7)(8)(9)(10)

SHITTY ———————————————————— AWESOME

THREE THINGS I'M **GRATEFUL FOR:**

_____
_____
_____
_____
_____
_____

REFLECTION OF YESTERDAY

DID I DO THE THINGS I **COMMITED** TO DO? (Y)(N)

DID I DO SOMETHING FOR **MYSELF**? (joy, rest, movement, fun) (Y)(N)

DID I PROTECT MY **ENERGY** AND SET **CLEAR BOUNDARIES**? (Y)(N)

DID I **CELEBRATE** A SMALL WIN (or acknowledge progress) (Y)(N)

DID I CHECK IN WITH MY **VISION + GOALS** (even briefly)? (Y)(N)

DID I MAKE AT LEAST ONE **BOLD MOVE** OR **CEO DECISION**? (Y)(N)

DID I **STAY FOCUSED** ON MY GROWTH? (Y)(N)

IF I ANSWERED "NO" TO ANY **WHAT DO I SHIFT TODAY**?

_____
_____
_____
_____

3 ACTION STEPS (COMMITMENTS) I WILL DO TODAY
THINGS YOU WILL COMMIT TO YOURSELF AND YOUR BUSINESS TO SUPPORT YOUR VISION

SOMETHING I NEED TO **REMIND MYSELF** OF TODAY _____

BUSINESS TO DO LIST:

PERSONAL TO DO LIST:

TOP PRIORITIES TODAY

_____

_____

_____

HOW MUCH **TIME** WILL I
DEDICATE TO MY BUSINESS
TODAY?

6 am

7 am

8 am

9 am

10 am

11 am

12 pm

1 pm

2 pm

3 pm

4 pm

5 pm

6 pm

7 pm

HOW WAS MY **SLEEP LAST NIGHT**

① ② ③ ④ ⑤ ⑥ ⑦ ⑧ ⑨ ⑩

HOW **MOTIVATED** DO I FEEL TODAY

① ② ③ ④ ⑤ ⑥ ⑦ ⑧ ⑨ ⑩

WHERE IS MY **PHYSICAL ENERGY LEVEL**

① ② ③ ④ ⑤ ⑥ ⑦ ⑧ ⑨ ⑩

HOW IS MY **EMOTIONAL CAPACITY**

① ② ③ ④ ⑤ ⑥ ⑦ ⑧ ⑨ ⑩

SHITTY ——————————————— AWESOME

THREE THINGS I'M GRATEFUL FOR:

_____

_____

_____

_____

_____

_____

REFLECTION OF YESTERDAY

DID I DO THE THINGS I **COMMITED** TO DO?	Y	N
DID I DO SOMETHING FOR **MYSELF**? (joy, rest, movement, fun)	Y	N
DID I PROTECT MY **ENERGY** AND SET **CLEAR BOUNDARIES**?	Y	N
DID I **CELEBRATE** A SMALL WIN (or acknowledge progress)	Y	N
DID I CHECK IN WITH MY **VISION + GOALS** (even briefly)?	Y	N
DID I MAKE AT LEAST ONE **BOLD MOVE** OR **CEO DECISION**?	Y	N
DID I **STAY FOCUSED** ON MY GROWTH?	Y	N

IF I ANSWERED "NO" TO ANY **WHAT DO I SHIFT TODAY**?

_____

_____

_____

_____

3 ACTION STEPS (COMMITMENTS) I WILL DO TODAY
THINGS YOU WILL COMMIT TO YOURSELF AND YOUR BUSINESS TO SUPPORT YOUR VISION

SOMETHING I NEED TO **REMIND MYSELF** OF TODAY _____

_____

BUSINESS TO DO LIST:

PERSONAL TO DO LIST:

TOP PRIORITIES TODAY

_____

_____

_____

HOW MUCH **TIME** WILL I DEDICATE TO MY BUSINESS TODAY?

6 am

7 am

8 am

9 am

10 am

11 am

12 pm

1 pm

2 pm

3 pm

4 pm

5 pm

6 pm

7 pm

HOW WAS MY **SLEEP LAST NIGHT**

1 2 3 4 5 6 7 8 9 10

HOW **MOTIVATED** DO I FEEL TODAY

1 2 3 4 5 6 7 8 9 10

WHERE IS MY **PHYSICAL ENERGY LEVEL**

1 2 3 4 5 6 7 8 9 10

HOW IS MY **EMOTIONAL CAPACITY**

1 2 3 4 5 6 7 8 9 10

SHITTY ———————————————— AWESOME

THREE THINGS I'M **GRATEFUL FOR:**

_____
_____
_____
_____
_____
_____
_____

REFLECTION OF YESTERDAY

DID I DO THE THINGS I **COMMITED** TO DO?   Y N

DID I DO SOMETHING FOR **MYSELF**? (joy, rest, movement, fun)   Y N

DID I PROTECT MY **ENERGY** AND SET **CLEAR BOUNDARIES**?   Y N

DID I **CELEBRATE** A SMALL WIN (or acknowledge progress)   Y N

DID I CHECK IN WITH MY **VISION + GOALS** (even briefly)?   Y N

DID I MAKE AT LEAST ONE **BOLD MOVE** OR **CEO DECISION**?   Y N

DID I **STAY FOCUSED** ON MY GROWTH?   Y N

IF I ANSWERED "NO" TO ANY **WHAT DO I SHIFT TODAY**?

_____
_____
_____
_____
_____

3 **ACTION STEPS** (COMMITMENTS) I WILL DO TODAY

THINGS YOU WILL COMMIT TO YOURSELF AND YOUR BUSINESS TO SUPPORT YOUR VISION

SOMETHING I NEED TO **REMIND MYSELF** OF TODAY _____

BUSINESS TO DO LIST:

PERSONAL TO DO LIST:

TOP PRIORITIES TODAY

_____

_____

_____

HOW MUCH **TIME** WILL I DEDICATE TO MY BUSINESS TODAY?

6 am

7 am

8 am

9 am

10 am

11 am

12 pm

1 pm

2 pm

3 pm

4 pm

5 pm

6 pm

7 pm

HOW WAS MY **SLEEP LAST NIGHT**

(1)(2)(3)(4)(5)(6)(7)(8)(9)(10)

HOW **MOTIVATED** DO I FEEL TODAY

(1)(2)(3)(4)(5)(6)(7)(8)(9)(10)

WHERE IS MY **PHYSICAL ENERGY LEVEL**

(1)(2)(3)(4)(5)(6)(7)(8)(9)(10)

HOW IS MY **EMOTIONAL CAPACITY**

(1)(2)(3)(4)(5)(6)(7)(8)(9)(10)

SHITTY ——————————————— AWESOME

THREE THINGS I'M
GRATEFUL FOR:

_____
_____
_____
_____
_____
_____
_____

REFLECTION OF YESTERDAY

DID I DO THE THINGS I **COMMITED** TO DO? (Y)(N)

DID I DO SOMETHING FOR **MYSELF**? (joy, rest, movement, fun) (Y)(N)

DID I PROTECT MY **ENERGY** AND SET **CLEAR BOUNDARIES**? (Y)(N)

DID I **CELEBRATE** A SMALL WIN (or acknowledge progress) (Y)(N)

DID I CHECK IN WITH MY **VISION + GOALS** (even briefly)? (Y)(N)

DID I MAKE AT LEAST ONE **BOLD MOVE** OR **CEO DECISION**? (Y)(N)

DID I **STAY FOCUSED** ON MY GROWTH? (Y)(N)

IF I ANSWERED "NO" TO ANY
WHAT DO I SHIFT TODAY?

_____
_____
_____
_____
_____

3 **ACTION STEPS** (COMMITMENTS) I WILL DO TODAY

THINGS YOU WILL COMMIT TO YOURSELF AND YOUR BUSINESS TO SUPPORT YOUR VISION

SOMETHING I NEED TO **REMIND MYSELF** OF TODAY _____

BUSINESS TO DO LIST:

PERSONAL TO DO LIST:

TOP PRIORITIES TODAY

_____

_____

_____

HOW MUCH **TIME** WILL I
DEDICATE TO MY BUSINESS
TODAY?

6 am

7 am

8 am

9 am

10 am

11 am

12 pm

1 pm

2 pm

3 pm

4 pm

5 pm

6 pm

7 pm

WEEKLY CHECK-IN

PERSONAL ENERGY & WELL-BEING
On a scale of 1–10, how would I rate...

MY OVERALL **ENERGY** THIS WEEK

① ② ③ ④ ⑤ ⑥ ⑦ ⑧ ⑨ ⑩

MY **EMOTIONAL CAPACITY** THIS WEEK

① ② ③ ④ ⑤ ⑥ ⑦ ⑧ ⑨ ⑩

MY **MOTIVATION + CLARITY** THIS WEEK

① ② ③ ④ ⑤ ⑥ ⑦ ⑧ ⑨ ⑩

SHITTY ———————————————— AWESOME

WHAT SUPPORTED MY WELL-BEING THIS WEEK?

_____

_____

WHAT DRAINED ME THAT I WANT TO SHIFT OR
ELIMINATE?

_____

_____

_____

WHAT DID I DO JUST FOR ME THIS WEEK?

_____

_____

BUSINESS & LEADERSHIP REFLECTIONS

DID I **STAY FOCUSED** ON MY TOP PRIORITIES? Ⓨ Ⓝ

DID I **LEAD** WITH CONFIDENCE, EVEN WHEN IT Ⓨ Ⓝ
WAS HARD?

DID I **SHOW UP** FOR MY BRAND IN A WAY I'M Ⓨ Ⓝ
PROUD OF?

DID I COMMUNICATE **CLEAR BOUNDARIES** Ⓨ Ⓝ
AROUND MY TIME?

WHAT WORKED REALLY WELL IN MY
BUSINESS THIS WEEK?

_____

WHAT CHALLENGES CAME UP, AND WHAT
DID I LEARN FROM THEM?

_____

WHAT BOLD MOVE DID I MAKE (OR WISH I
HAD)?

_____

ALIGNMENT & INTENTION

AM I STILL MOVING TOWARD MY BIGGER
VISION — OR AM I JUST STAYING BUSY?

WHAT DO I NEED TO PAUSE, PIVOT, OR
RELEASE RIGHT NOW?

WHAT'S ONE THING I WANT TO RECOMMIT
TO NEXT WEEK?

NEXT WEEK'S FOCUS

ONE BOLD THING I'LL DO THIS WEEK

ONE BOUNDARY I'LL PROTECT

WEEKLY **GOAL PLANNER** LIKE A
DAMN BUSINESS BADASS

MY **WEEKLY** FOCUS

TOP 3 POWER GOALS FOR THIS WEEK - (WHAT ACTUALLY MOVES THE NEEDLE — NOT BUSY WORK.)

ENERGY + MINDSET FOCUS:

(ONE VIBE, MANTRA, OR ENERGY YOU'RE CHOOSING TO LEAD WITH THIS WEEK.) _____

CELEBRATE YOUR DAMN WINS:

INNER WINS **(MINDSET + ENERGY)**	**ACTION WINS** **(SH*T YOU ACTUALLY DID)**	**ALIGNMENT WINS** **(SOUL-LEVEL YES MOMENTS)**
THE MOMENTS YOU CHOSE GROWTH, CALM, COURAGE, OR CLARITY OVER CHAOS.	TANGIBLE MOVES YOU MADE — BIG OR SMALL — THAT PROVE YOU'RE BUILDING MOMENTUM.	WHEN SOMETHING FELT RIGHT, EASY, ALIGNED, OR JOYFULLY YOU.

WHAT NEEDS TO **SHIFT** ASAP?

HOW WAS MY **SLEEP LAST NIGHT**

(1) (2) (3) (4) (5) (6) (7) (8) (9) (10)

HOW **MOTIVATED** DO I FEEL TODAY

(1) (2) (3) (4) (5) (6) (7) (8) (9) (10)

WHERE IS MY **PHYSICAL ENERGY LEVEL**

(1) (2) (3) (4) (5) (6) (7) (8) (9) (10)

HOW IS MY **EMOTIONAL CAPACITY**

(1) (2) (3) (4) (5) (6) (7) (8) (9) (10)

SHITTY ———————————————— AWESOME

THREE THINGS I'M GRATEFUL FOR:

_____
_____
_____
_____
_____
_____
_____

REFLECTION OF YESTERDAY

DID I DO THE THINGS I **COMMITED** TO DO? (Y) (N)

DID I DO SOMETHING FOR **MYSELF**? (joy, rest, movement, fun) (Y) (N)

DID I PROTECT MY **ENERGY** AND SET **CLEAR BOUNDARIES**? (Y) (N)

DID I **CELEBRATE** A SMALL WIN (or acknowledge progress) (Y) (N)

DID I CHECK IN WITH MY **VISION + GOALS** (even briefly)? (Y) (N)

DID I MAKE AT LEAST ONE **BOLD MOVE** OR **CEO DECISION**? (Y) (N)

DID I **STAY FOCUSED** ON MY GROWTH? (Y) (N)

IF I ANSWERED "NO" TO ANY **WHAT DO I SHIFT TODAY**?

_____
_____
_____
_____
_____

3 **ACTION STEPS** (COMMITMENTS) I WILL DO TODAY

THINGS YOU WILL COMMIT TO YOURSELF AND YOUR BUSINESS TO SUPPORT YOUR VISION

SOMETHING I NEED TO **REMIND MYSELF** OF TODAY _____

BUSINESS TO DO LIST:

PERSONAL TO DO LIST:

TOP PRIORITIES TODAY

_____

_____

_____

_____

HOW MUCH **TIME** WILL I
DEDICATE TO MY BUSINESS
TODAY?

6 am

7 am

8 am

9 am

10 am

11 am

12 pm

1 pm

2 pm

3 pm

4 pm

5 pm

6 pm

7 pm

HOW WAS MY **SLEEP LAST NIGHT**

1 2 3 4 5 6 7 8 9 10

HOW **MOTIVATED** DO I FEEL TODAY

1 2 3 4 5 6 7 8 9 10

WHERE IS MY **PHYSICAL ENERGY LEVEL**

1 2 3 4 5 6 7 8 9 10

HOW IS MY **EMOTIONAL CAPACITY**

1 2 3 4 5 6 7 8 9 10

SHITTY ———————————————— AWESOME

THREE THINGS I'M **GRATEFUL FOR:**

_____
_____
_____
_____
_____
_____
_____

REFLECTION OF YESTERDAY

	Y / N
DID I DO THE THINGS I **COMMITED** TO DO?	Y N
DID I DO SOMETHING FOR **MYSELF**? (joy, rest, movement, fun)	Y N
DID I PROTECT MY **ENERGY** AND SET **CLEAR BOUNDARIES**?	Y N
DID I **CELEBRATE** A SMALL WIN (or acknowledge progress)	Y N
DID I CHECK IN WITH MY **VISION + GOALS** (even briefly)?	Y N
DID I MAKE AT LEAST ONE **BOLD MOVE** OR **CEO DECISION**?	Y N
DID I **STAY FOCUSED** ON MY GROWTH?	Y N

IF I ANSWERED "NO" TO ANY
WHAT DO I SHIFT TODAY?

_____
_____
_____
_____
_____

3 **ACTION STEPS** (COMMITMENTS) I WILL DO TODAY
THINGS YOU WILL COMMIT TO YOURSELF AND YOUR BUSINESS TO SUPPORT YOUR VISION

SOMETHING I NEED TO **REMIND MYSELF** OF TODAY _____

BUSINESS TO DO LIST:

PERSONAL TO DO LIST:

TOP PRIORITIES TODAY

_____

_____

_____

_____

HOW MUCH **TIME** WILL I
DEDICATE TO MY BUSINESS
TODAY?

6 am

7 am

8 am

9 am

10 am

11 am

12 pm

1 pm

2 pm

3 pm

4 pm

5 pm

6 pm

7 pm

HOW WAS MY **SLEEP LAST NIGHT**

(1) (2) (3) (4) (5) (6) (7) (8) (9) (10)

HOW **MOTIVATED** DO I FEEL TODAY

(1) (2) (3) (4) (5) (6) (7) (8) (9) (10)

WHERE IS MY **PHYSICAL ENERGY LEVEL**

(1) (2) (3) (4) (5) (6) (7) (8) (9) (10)

HOW IS MY **EMOTIONAL CAPACITY**

(1) (2) (3) (4) (5) (6) (7) (8) (9) (10)

SHITTY ——————————————— AWESOME

THREE THINGS I'M **GRATEFUL FOR:**

_____
_____
_____
_____
_____
_____
_____
_____
_____

REFLECTION OF YESTERDAY

DID I DO THE THINGS I **COMMITED** TO DO? (Y) (N)

DID I DO SOMETHING FOR **MYSELF**? (joy, rest, movement, fun) (Y) (N)

DID I PROTECT MY **ENERGY** AND SET **CLEAR BOUNDARIES**? (Y) (N)

DID I **CELEBRATE** A SMALL WIN (or acknowledge progress) (Y) (N)

DID I CHECK IN WITH MY **VISION + GOALS** (even briefly)? (Y) (N)

DID I MAKE AT LEAST ONE **BOLD MOVE** OR **CEO DECISION**? (Y) (N)

DID I **STAY FOCUSED** ON MY GROWTH? (Y) (N)

IF I ANSWERED "NO" TO ANY **WHAT DO I SHIFT TODAY**?

_____
_____
_____
_____
_____

3 **ACTION STEPS** (COMMITMENTS) I WILL DO TODAY

THINGS YOU WILL COMMIT TO YOURSELF AND YOUR BUSINESS TO SUPPORT YOUR VISION

SOMETHING I NEED TO **REMIND MYSELF** OF TODAY _____

BUSINESS TO DO LIST:

PERSONAL TO DO LIST:

TOP PRIORITIES TODAY

_____

_____

_____

_____

HOW MUCH **TIME** WILL I DEDICATE TO MY BUSINESS TODAY?

6 am

7 am

8 am

9 am

10 am

11 am

12 pm

1 pm

2 pm

3 pm

4 pm

5 pm

6 pm

7 pm

She's the STRATEGY

HOW WAS MY SLEEP LAST NIGHT

(1) (2) (3) (4) (5) (6) (7) (8) (9) (10)

HOW MOTIVATED DO I FEEL TODAY

(1) (2) (3) (4) (5) (6) (7) (8) (9) (10)

WHERE IS MY PHYSICAL ENERGY LEVEL

(1) (2) (3) (4) (5) (6) (7) (8) (9) (10)

HOW IS MY EMOTIONAL CAPACITY

(1) (2) (3) (4) (5) (6) (7) (8) (9) (10)

SHITTY ———————————————— AWESOME

THREE THINGS I'M GRATEFUL FOR:

_____
_____
_____
_____
_____
_____

REFLECTION OF YESTERDAY

DID I DO THE THINGS I **COMMITED** TO DO? (Y) (N)

DID I DO SOMETHING FOR **MYSELF**? (joy, rest, movement, fun) (Y) (N)

DID I PROTECT MY **ENERGY** AND SET **CLEAR BOUNDARIES**? (Y) (N)

DID I **CELEBRATE** A SMALL WIN (or acknowledge progress) (Y) (N)

DID I CHECK IN WITH MY **VISION + GOALS** (even briefly)? (Y) (N)

DID I MAKE AT LEAST ONE **BOLD MOVE** OR **CEO DECISION**? (Y) (N)

DID I **STAY FOCUSED** ON MY GROWTH? (Y) (N)

IF I ANSWERED "NO" TO ANY **WHAT DO I SHIFT TODAY**?

_____
_____
_____
_____
_____

---

3 ACTION STEPS (COMMITMENTS) I WILL DO TODAY
THINGS YOU WILL COMMIT TO YOURSELF AND YOUR BUSINESS TO SUPPORT YOUR VISION

SOMETHING I NEED TO **REMIND MYSELF** OF TODAY _____

BUSINESS TO DO LIST:

PERSONAL TO DO LIST:

TOP PRIORITIES TODAY

_____
_____
_____
_____

HOW MUCH **TIME** WILL I DEDICATE TO MY BUSINESS TODAY?

6 am

7 am

8 am

9 am

10 am

11 am

12 pm

1 pm

2 pm

3 pm

4 pm

5 pm

6 pm

7 pm

HOW WAS MY **SLEEP LAST NIGHT**

(1) (2) (3) (4) (5) (6) (7) (8) (9) (10)

HOW **MOTIVATED** DO I FEEL TODAY

(1) (2) (3) (4) (5) (6) (7) (8) (9) (10)

WHERE IS MY **PHYSICAL ENERGY LEVEL**

(1) (2) (3) (4) (5) (6) (7) (8) (9) (10)

HOW IS MY **EMOTIONAL CAPACITY**

(1) (2) (3) (4) (5) (6) (7) (8) (9) (10)

SHITTY —————————————————————— AWESOME

THREE THINGS I'M **GRATEFUL FOR:**

_____
_____
_____
_____
_____
_____
_____

REFLECTION OF YESTERDAY

DID I DO THE THINGS I **COMMITED** TO DO? (Y) (N)

DID I DO SOMETHING FOR **MYSELF**? (joy, rest, movement, fun) (Y) (N)

DID I PROTECT MY **ENERGY** AND SET **CLEAR BOUNDARIES**? (Y) (N)

DID I **CELEBRATE** A SMALL WIN (or acknowledge progress) (Y) (N)

DID I CHECK IN WITH MY **VISION + GOALS** (even briefly)? (Y) (N)

DID I MAKE AT LEAST ONE **BOLD MOVE** OR **CEO DECISION**? (Y) (N)

DID I **STAY FOCUSED** ON MY GROWTH? (Y) (N)

IF I ANSWERED "NO" TO ANY **WHAT DO I SHIFT TODAY**?

_____
_____
_____
_____
_____

---

3 ACTION STEPS (COMMITMENTS) I WILL DO TODAY
THINGS YOU WILL COMMIT TO YOURSELF AND YOUR BUSINESS TO SUPPORT YOUR VISION

SOMETHING I NEED TO **REMIND MYSELF** OF TODAY _____

BUSINESS TO DO LIST:

PERSONAL TO DO LIST:

TOP PRIORITIES TODAY

_____

_____

_____

_____

HOW MUCH **TIME** WILL I
DEDICATE TO MY BUSINESS
TODAY?

6 am

7 am

8 am

9 am

10 am

11 am

12 pm

1 pm

2 pm

3 pm

4 pm

5 pm

6 pm

7 pm

JAN   FEB   MAR   APR   MAY   JUN   JUL   AUG   SEP   OCT   NOV   DEC   20____
1 2 3 4 5 6 7 8 9 10 11 12 13 14 15 16 17 18 19 20 21 22 23 24 25 26 27 28 29 30 31

HOW WAS MY **SLEEP LAST NIGHT**

① ② ③ ④ ⑤ ⑥ ⑦ ⑧ ⑨ ⑩

HOW **MOTIVATED** DO I FEEL TODAY

① ② ③ ④ ⑤ ⑥ ⑦ ⑧ ⑨ ⑩

WHERE IS MY **PHYSICAL ENERGY LEVEL**

① ② ③ ④ ⑤ ⑥ ⑦ ⑧ ⑨ ⑩

HOW IS MY **EMOTIONAL CAPACITY**

① ② ③ ④ ⑤ ⑥ ⑦ ⑧ ⑨ ⑩

SHITTY ————————————————— AWESOME

THREE THINGS I'M **GRATEFUL FOR:**

_____
_____
_____
_____
_____
_____

REFLECTION OF YESTERDAY

DID I DO THE THINGS I **COMMITED** TO DO?   Ⓨ Ⓝ

DID I DO SOMETHING FOR **MYSELF**? (joy, rest, movement, fun)   Ⓨ Ⓝ

DID I PROTECT MY **ENERGY** AND SET **CLEAR BOUNDARIES**?   Ⓨ Ⓝ

DID I **CELEBRATE** A SMALL WIN (or acknowledge progress)   Ⓨ Ⓝ

DID I CHECK IN WITH MY **VISION + GOALS** (even briefly)?   Ⓨ Ⓝ

DID I MAKE AT LEAST ONE **BOLD MOVE** OR **CEO DECISION**?   Ⓨ Ⓝ

DID I **STAY FOCUSED** ON MY GROWTH?   Ⓨ Ⓝ

IF I ANSWERED "NO" TO ANY **WHAT DO I SHIFT TODAY**?

_____
_____
_____
_____
_____

3 ACTION STEPS (COMMITMENTS) I WILL DO TODAY
THINGS YOU WILL COMMIT TO YOURSELF AND YOUR BUSINESS TO SUPPORT YOUR VISION

SOMETHING I NEED TO **REMIND MYSELF** OF TODAY _____

BUSINESS TO DO LIST:

PERSONAL TO DO LIST:

TOP PRIORITIES TODAY

_____

_____

_____

_____

HOW MUCH **TIME** WILL I DEDICATE TO MY BUSINESS TODAY?

6 am

7 am

8 am

9 am

10 am

11 am

12 pm

1 pm

2 pm

3 pm

4 pm

5 pm

6 pm

7 pm

She's the
STRATEGY
Unapologetically Authentic. Own That Damn Business

JAN   FEB   MAR   APR   MAY   JUN   JUL   AUG   SEP   OCT   NOV   DEC   20___
1   2   3   4   5   6   7   8   9   10   11   12   13   14   15   16   17   18   19   20   21   22   23   24   25   26   27   28   29   30   31

HOW WAS MY **SLEEP LAST NIGHT**

① ② ③ ④ ⑤ ⑥ ⑦ ⑧ ⑨ ⑩

HOW **MOTIVATED** DO I FEEL TODAY

① ② ③ ④ ⑤ ⑥ ⑦ ⑧ ⑨ ⑩

WHERE IS MY **PHYSICAL ENERGY LEVEL**

① ② ③ ④ ⑤ ⑥ ⑦ ⑧ ⑨ ⑩

HOW IS MY **EMOTIONAL CAPACITY**

① ② ③ ④ ⑤ ⑥ ⑦ ⑧ ⑨ ⑩

SHITTY ———————————————————— AWESOME

THREE THINGS I'M GRATEFUL FOR:

_____

_____

_____

_____

_____

_____

REFLECTION OF YESTERDAY

DID I DO THE THINGS I **COMMITED** TO DO? (Y)(N)

DID I DO SOMETHING FOR **MYSELF**? (joy, rest, movement, fun) (Y)(N)

DID I PROTECT MY **ENERGY** AND SET **CLEAR BOUNDARIES**? (Y)(N)

DID I **CELEBRATE** A SMALL WIN (or acknowledge progress) (Y)(N)

DID I CHECK IN WITH MY **VISION + GOALS** (even briefly)? (Y)(N)

DID I MAKE AT LEAST ONE **BOLD MOVE** OR **CEO DECISION**? (Y)(N)

DID I **STAY FOCUSED** ON MY GROWTH? (Y)(N)

IF I ANSWERED "NO" TO ANY
WHAT DO I SHIFT TODAY?

_____

_____

_____

_____

_____

3 **ACTION STEPS** (COMMITMENTS) I WILL DO TODAY
THINGS YOU WILL COMMIT TO YOURSELF AND YOUR BUSINESS TO SUPPORT YOUR VISION

SOMETHING I NEED TO **REMIND MYSELF** OF TODAY _____

_____

BUSINESS TO DO LIST:

PERSONAL TO DO LIST:

TOP PRIORITIES TODAY

_____

_____

_____

HOW MUCH **TIME** WILL I
DEDICATE TO MY BUSINESS
TODAY?

6 am

7 am

8 am

9 am

10 am

11 am

12 pm

1 pm

2 pm

3 pm

4 pm

5 pm

6 pm

7 pm

MONTHLY CHECK-IN

A MOMENT TO ZOOM OUT, REALIGN, AND POWER UP.

MONTHLY WINS

MY **PROUDEST** MOMENT

A MILESTONE I **REACHED** (BIG OR SMALL):

A CHALLENGE I **OVERCAME**

BY THE **NUMBERS**

CLIENTS SERVED: _____

REVENUE/INCOME: _____

OFFERS PROMOTED/LAUNCHED: _____

PERSONAL REFLECTION

I FELT LIKE THE CEO OF MY LIFE Ⓨ Ⓝ

I TOOK CARE OF MYSELF CONSISTENTLY Ⓨ Ⓝ

I FELT ALIGNED WITH MY BUSINESS VISION: Ⓨ Ⓝ

WHAT DID I LEARN ABOUT MYSELF THIS MONTH? _____

WHAT DO I WANT TO CELEBRATE MORE OFTEN? _____

WHAT BELIEF OR HABIT NEEDS TO SHIFT NEXT MONTH? _____

RESET + **RECOMMIT**

WHAT WILL I TAKE WITH ME INTO NEXT MONTH?

WHAT WILL I LEAVE BEHIND WITH?

WHAT DO I WANT TO EXPERIENCE MORE OF?

MY **FOCUS THEME** FOR **NEXT MONTH**: _____

MONTHLY **GOAL PLANNER** LIKE A
DAMN BUSINESS BADASS

MY **MONTHLY** FOCUS

MONTH: _____

WHAT SPECIFIC OUTCOME DO I WANT TO CREATE BY THE END OF THIS MONTH?

MY **MEASURABLE** GOAL
(CLIENT COUNT, REVENUE TARGET, AUDIENCE GROWTH, ETC.) _____

_____

MY SUPPORT SYSTEM	**MY SELF-CARE STRATEGY**	**VISION BUILDER**
WHAT SUPPORT, TOOLS, OR PEOPLE DO I NEED TO HELP ME MOVE FORWARD?	WHAT WILL BALANCE, REST, OR JOY LOOK LIKE THIS MONTH?	WHO AM I BECOMING IN THIS BUSINESS?

QUARTER: **Q1 / Q2 / Q3 / Q4** (CIRCLE ONE)

YEAR: _____

IF I FULLY TRUSTED MYSELF, WHAT WOULD I CREATE OR LAUNCH THIS QUARTER? _____

WHAT DOES SUCCESS LOOK AND FEEL LIKE TO ME (NOT SOCIETY'S VERSION)? _____

WHAT DO I WANT TO BE KNOWN FOR BY THE END OF THIS QUARTER?

She's the
STRATEGY
Unapologetically Authentic. Own That Damn Business.

BEING **FUCKING ACCOUNTABLE** LIKE A
DAMN BUSINESS BADASS

Look — you didn't come this far just to fill in some pretty pages and call it growth. You came to build. To lead. To rise. And now? It's time to hold yourself to that next-level standard — like a CEO who's DONE playing small.

This is where mindset meets momentum. Where action becomes identity. Where you stop hoping — and start moving like the boss you're becoming.

Because let's be real...Accountability is your accelerator. Support is your shortcut. Strategy is your secret weapon.

READY FOR THE REAL MAGIC? If you loved this workbook, babe — you're just getting started.

Come find me online for:

- ✅ ONLINE COACHING PROGRAMS
- ✅ GROUP MENTORSHIP EXPERIENCES
- ✅ 1:1 BUSINESS DEEP-DIVES
- ✅ TOOLS THAT'LL KEEP YOU LIT UP + LOCKED IN

She'sTheStrategy.com

Let's keep building your brand, your confidence, your empire — together.

You're not just a dreamer. You're a damn builder. Now act like it.

www.ingramcontent.com/pod-product-compliance
Lightning Source LLC
Chambersburg PA
CBHW041137120626
46547CB00020B/3027